Advance Praise for

Slow Family Living

"In a society set on having it all, *Slow Family Living* points out: Wait! You already have what you need. All you have to do is slow down and appreciate it. Bernadette Noll's book helps us reject the time- and money-wasters we've been sold on, and savor the most golden thing we've got—time, especially time together."

—Lenore Skenazy, author of *Free-Range Kids*

"Bernadette Noll has a long track record of helping families slow down and find the pace of life that suits them best. How lucky we are that she has now distilled her experience into a wise and readable book. *Slow Family Living* is packed with practical ways to bring joy and sanity back to family life and give our children a childhood worthy of the name. In this overstimulated, crazy-busy, roadrunner culture of ours, every family needs a copy."

—Carl Honoré, author of *In Praise of Slow* and *Under Pressure*

"Slowing down and making time for the gestation of your own ideas and being conscious of your own process are the foundations of both genius and happiness. Rather than letting the pace of the world determine your own family's pace, *Slow Family Living* encourages everyone to step back from the craziness and determine their own rhythms and routines. The pauses are integral not only to happiness but to pure unadulterated brilliance."

—Gever Tulley, author of *50 Dangerous Things*
(You Should Let Your Children Do)

continued . . .

"Bernadette Noll, one of my favorite authors, offers essential advice for healthy family living: Slow down and be present with yourself and your loved ones. Her 75 'recipes' for slow family living are down-to-earth and easy to implement. This book is a real gem, a peaceful haven in a sea of overstimulation."

—Peggy O'Mara, founder of Mothering.com

Parents Praise the Slow Family Living Movement

"So much fantastic, useful and inspiring information! Thanks!"

—S.W., Edmonton, AB

"Raising emotionally whole, healthy people is no easy task. It does take a village as well as a lot of time and energy. I applaud this movement to slow down and see what is really important."

—A.M., Portland, ME

"If you want to do something to change the world for the better and really understand why you're the kind of parent you are: take this class."

—E.B., Austin, TX

Slow
Family
Living

75 Simple Ways to
Slow Down, Connect, and
Create More Joy

Bernadette Noll

A PERIGEE BOOK

A PERIGEE BOOK
Published by the Penguin Group
Penguin Group (USA) Inc.
375 Hudson Street, New York, New York 10014, USA

Penguin Group (Canada), 90 Eglinton Avenue East, Suite 700, Toronto, Ontario M4P 2Y3, Canada
(a division of Pearson Penguin Canada Inc.) • Penguin Books Ltd., 80 Strand, London WC2R 0RL,
England • Penguin Ireland, 25 St. Stephen's Green, Dublin 2, Ireland (a division of Penguin
Books Ltd.) • Penguin Group (Australia), 707 Collins Street, Melbourne, Victoria 3008, Australia
(a division of Pearson Australia Group Pty Ltd.) • Penguin Books India Pvt. Ltd., 11 Community
Centre, Panchsheel Park, New Delhi—110 017, India • Penguin Group (NZ), 67 Apollo Drive,
Rosedale, Auckland 0632, New Zealand (a division of Pearson New Zealand Ltd.) •
Penguin Books (South Africa), Rosebank Office Park, 181 Jan Smuts Avenue,
Parktown North 2193, South Africa • Penguin China, B7 Jiaming Center,
27 East Third Ring Road North, Chaoyang District, Beijing 100020, China
Penguin Books Ltd., Registered Offices: 80 Strand, London WC2R 0RL, England

While the author has made every effort to provide accurate telephone numbers, Internet addresses, and
other contact information at the time of publication, neither the publisher nor the author assumes any
responsibility for errors, or for changes that occur after publication. Further, the publisher does not have any
control over and does not assume any responsibility for author or third-party websites or their content.

First edition: March 2013

Library of Congress Cataloging-in-Publication Data

Noll, Bernadette.
Slow family living : 75 simple ways to slow down, connect, and create more joy / Bernadette Noll.
pages   cm
ISBN 978-0-399-16007-3
1. Families.   2. Parenthood.   3. Parent and child.   I. Title.
HQ755.8.N59846   2013
306.85—dc23   2012040601

PRINTED IN THE UNITED STATES OF AMERICA

10   9   8   7   6   5   4   3   2   1

Most Perigee books are available at special quantity discounts for bulk purchases
for sales promotions, premiums, fund-raising, or educational use. Special books, or book
excerpts, can also be created to fit specific needs. For details, write: Special Markets,
Penguin Group (USA) Inc., 375 Hudson Street, New York, New York 10014.

To Kenny. Thank you for being.

Contents

CONTENTS

CONTENTS

Foreword

What do humans need to be healthy, whole, and connected?

This is a question I've been asking myself since childhood. As an adult I've created a professional life that affords me the opportunity to work with thousands of families. I have created my own laboratory, under the auspices of being an early parenting coach and human development specialist, which allows me to explore this very question. However, this is not an exploration that started in adulthood.

As a very young person I was drawn to babies and children. As a result, I spent a lot of time with the moms in my neighborhood as a mother's helper. I would spend hours in their homes watching them parent their children and talking to them about life and motherhood. Little did I know then I was studying and gathering information that would serve me professionally down the road. They lived slow, connected, joyful lives. It felt right being with them. It felt like life was safe and flowing, and well paced. I definitely tucked that away in my subconscious.

As my path unfolded I became fascinated with psychology and later, holistic health. The same question kept coming up over and over and over again, What do humans need to be healthy, whole, and connected?

My quest continued and I stumbled on the field of prenatal and perinatal psychology. The field draws from research and theory in the areas of cellular biology, attachment theory, interpersonal neurobiology, epigenetics, and consciousness studies and is based on the premise that we arrive as whole, conscious beings in very immature, very vulnerable, bodies. From this perspective, development is viewed not as a process of pouring information in but rather as a process of unfolding out into our best and most expansive selves. And this takes time and care and lots of love.

So where does slowing down fit into all of this? It's a necessary part of human development. As we take in all of the information that is thrown our way, day in and day out, it is absolutely necessary for us to pause long enough for our brains to absorb and integrate all that we have seen, heard, and learned in the course of a day—whether that is information or relationships. We thrive when we are taking in and then pausing to integrate. Doing and then being. Doing, being. Doing, being. When we do this, we stay emotionally and physiologically resourced. When we are resourced we are more present, more compassionate, more connected. We navigate life in more fluid and relaxed ways. When we don't allow for the pauses that are essential to healthy humanhood, we get overwhelmed. When we are in constant go, go, go mode we are stressing our systems in a way that can leave us physically and emotionally exhausted and disconnected— with ourselves and the people around us.

This is especially true for children who are constantly introduced to so many new things as they move through their world. If we rush ourselves from event to activity, from lesson to obligation, and from there to homework, chores, and more, then there is no time for the integration of it all. Slowing down is a crucial part of the assimilation of all the information and personal encounters we make in a day. Both in the family and out. So, it's more than just a good idea, it's a crucial element of living life to the very fullest!

So, what do humans need to be healthy, whole, and connected? From my perspective, it's really quite simple:

Slow down.

Connect.

Enjoy.

I assume you are reading this book because you are interested in creating a slower, more connected, joy-filled family life. Well, you've come to the right place. This book will give you the information, tools, and inspiration to do just that. Bernadette is a constant student and teacher of this way of being. She's not here to tell you how to do it, rather to offer ideas and suggestions and to guide you in finding the way that works best for you. And I believe that is as good as it gets. Enjoy!

THE BENEFITS OF SLOW

* When you slow down family life, you're able to stay more resourced.

* When you are more resourced, you are more present.

* When you are more present, you are more tuned into your own needs and the needs of everyone in the family.

* When you are more tuned into the needs of each individual, everyone feels seen.

* When everyone feels seen, everyone feels safe.

* When everyone feels safe, there is more harmony.

* When there is more harmony, there is more love, more connection, more ease, more fun, and more joy.

* When there is more love, connection, ease, fun, and joy, there's more desire to be together as a family!

* Now and forever.

—Carrie Contey, PhD
Summer 2012

What Is Slow Family Living?

The basic tenets of Slow Family Living are simple: slow down, connect, and enjoy family life. In the face of society's messages, however, to speed up, sign up, join up, and *hurry up*, the reality can be a bit more difficult to achieve without a little guidance. This is where the idea was born.

For every new parent, the message from parents of older children is clear, "Enjoy it now as childhood is fleeting. Before you know it your kids will be off in the world, and you'll be wondering how it all happened so fast." For new parents, muddling through the minutiae of raising small children, this is hard to fathom. And yet, at the same time, the message from society seems to be that raising small children is merely something to endure. And as children enter school, time flies even faster, and society's rules and messages can take over, leaving no room at all for connection and enjoyment of the family we created.

This is where Slow Family Living comes in. We want to give families permission to step back from the dogma, tune out society's have-tos and must-haves, and tune into their own gut and their own family members to live a slower, more fun, more connected family life—now and for the long haul, because as parents we have our children as adults for *way* longer than we have them as children. Though raising a family isn't always fun and games, we can make it so that joy and connection are the baseline we can return to time and time again. Sometimes it's in a method, and other times it's simply in the mind-set; with this book I aim to offer both.

Slow is not about doing nothing all the time, though some afternoons that might be exactly what you need and choose to do. Rather slow is in the connections made and the mindfulness of the process. Slow is in the pause taken throughout the days, weeks, months, and years to ponder exactly what you want from family life and how you want it to feel. And slow is in making sure that what you do in the day-to-day brings you the human connection you desire for the years to come.

Most parents, when asked to look down the parenting road twenty years from now, say their greatest hope is for a meaningful relationship with their kids. Slow Family Living is about creating that relationship now—while the children are home, while dinner is being made, while the carpool is forming, and while the laundry's getting folded. Slow Family Living is about stepping away from the busyness of life, sometimes for just minutes at a time, and finding each other in all you do so that you can have each other down the road.

Slow Family Living is about believing that family life can be the well, rather than the drain. That family life can be the place where we go to fill up, find ideas and inspiration, seek comfort and ease, and become our truest and best selves.

Slow Family Living is the desire for and discovery of ways to see and hear each member as an individual while simultaneously seeing the family as an entity. Slow is in finding presence— with yourself, with each family member, and with the family as a whole so that connection and joy are an integral part of the experience.

Slow Family Living is about taking the time to ask what do we need and want, as humans and members of this family. In the answer lies the slow, connected, and more joyful family life, now and twenty, thirty, forty years down the road. It is the goal of Slow Family Living to help families find presence now, to find joy now, and to find connection now so that it can exist for all time.

How Did It All Begin?

In January 2007, Carrie Contey, PhD, and I began holding classes and leading workshops with families who were seeking to foster a greater connection within family life. They were tired of being on the proverbial treadmill—running from thing to thing and event to event, and feeling that family life always came last. They were tired too of questioning this desire they had in the face of society's pressure to join in, sign up, and do more. After an in-depth workshop with several families who were struggling to answer the question, What do we want out of family life? we realized what was needed was something akin to slow food, a way for families to connect with the process of living family life. A way for the process to be given space and to be thoughtful and fun. That afternoon we wrote the manifesto for Slow Family Living—or rather the manifesto came our way; the ideas presented themselves, and a movement was born.

We began holding classes around this theme. We built a community of interested families who came together for family park days and online in our virtual community at SlowFamily Living.com. We have given myriad workshops and talks to help families find their own version of slow and have answered questions from families as close as Austin and as far away as Australia and Europe and Asia. We created workbooks to help families find their own slow, and the concept grew into a way of life.

The **slow** is in the pause. The deep breath. The pondering. The examining.

The **connect** is in the eye contact. In the transitions. In the chores. In the downtime and the crazy times. And in the intention added to each moment.

And the **joy** is in the decision to make it fun. Find pleasure in the minutiae even if it means laughing at the absurdity of it all. For now. And for our whole lives long.

I wrote this book not as dogma, or another trend you should follow, but rather as an offering of ideas, of serving suggestions for some things you can do to build the joy and connection you want. Like a cookbook, I hope you take these ideas and mix them with the ingredients and tastes you have in your own home and in your own family.

However you do it is up to you. My wish is that it brings you slowness, connection, and joy with your family.

Before Slow Family

In the foreword, Carrie told you her tale of how she came to this slow family table. And where her desire came from to help families find ways to slow down, connect, and enjoy family life.

My story is different but just as steeped in my personal history.

I grew up in New Jersey as one of nine siblings, and to this day my siblings and my parents are some of my favorite people in this world. They are the ones I call for advice, information, and consolation and to share something funny, sad, or bittersweet. My parents gave us an enjoyment of each other and a sense of feeling connected to the tribe that is our immediate and extended family. It is, without a doubt, a lucky and loving existence.

This is not to say that it was without strife or arguing or disagreement or hurt—but after all that, there was the knowledge that forgiveness was readily available and understanding and kindness, too.

After my husband, Kenny, and I had our own children, we wanted very much for them to have that same bond with each other and with us. It is our hope and our intention that they think about family life as connection, fun, exploration, safety, love, understanding, forgiveness, and all the other things that make it a little easier to walk this life of ours.

Someone once referred to me as a "parenting expert." That I am truly not. What I am is a perpetual student of it all—of parenting and partnering and friendship and compassion and of living the most joyful, connected life I can possibly live.

What's in This Book?

In the pages that follow, you'll find seventy-five suggestions for ways to slow down, connect, and find joy in life's everyday moments. Some of the ideas are anecdotes from our own lives, some are ideas from other families, and still others are questions to get you thinking about what you want your family life to look and feel like. Some are methods, and some are mind-sets.

I hope you find some ideas in here that work for you. I hope that they inspire you to try something new, and I hope too that you can take them and tweak them to build more joy and connection for your own family.

If you want to read more about Slow Family Living or about me or contact me with a question, you can find me at Slow FamilyLiving.com.

The Slow Family Manifesto

Slow Family Living is a revolution in the way we think about, embrace, and implement family living.

It was born out of our belief that family life is being hijacked by societal messages that more is better and faster is greater and that you and your children are at risk of being left behind, unless you buy in *now*.

It is about checking in with yourself. It is about allowing family life to unfold in a way that is joyfully and consciously connected. This means slowing it down, finding comfort in the home, and creating the space to see and honor the family as an entity, while simultaneously keeping sight of each member as a unique and valuable individual.

Slow Family Living believes that family life can serve as the incubator for deeper compassion, creativity, love, harmony, humor, appreciation, respect, fun, ingenuity, conflict resolution, peace, friendship, growth, communication, and perhaps above all else, true, unending, and powerful joy.

As we intentionally give value and space to family life, we are thereby creating a force—with a sum greater than its parts—that can then flow out into the local and the global communities.

Slow Family Living holds this as truth: The peace and harmony we want to exist within the world can be created within the family first, by bringing it home and lovingly, consciously, and intentionally slowing life down.

SLOW FAMILY LIVING IS . . .

* Doing things you love

* Knowing you have choices

* Consciously making decisions

* Doing things because it brings more connection

* Doing things because it feels right for your family

* Taking into consideration each family member and their stage of development

* Making the family unit your priority

* Sometimes taking a stand against the status quo

* Possibly doing it differently from the way it was done for you

* Asking yourself over and over again, Is this working for us?

* Trusting that what you have to offer your family right now is enough

* Trusting that there's no right way to do it, just the way that feels right for you and your family

* Pausing as a unit to stop and take it all in

* Being present in the moments

* Getting connected to your emotions and encouraging and teaching your family members to do the same

* Defining success for yourself

* Being willing to shift gears when you need to

* Celebrating the moments

SLOW FAMILY LIVING IS NOT . . .

* A prescription for living

* Doing it somebody else's way

* More dogma

* Doing it because it's what you're supposed to do

* Doing it because it's the way it's always been done

* Necessarily what everybody else is doing

* About getting ahead

* Using someone else's definition of success

* Inactivity or indecision

75 Ways to

Slow Down

Together

1

Is This Working for Us?

At the core of Slow Family Living is the question *Is this working for us?* It is the question that can bring us to more joy, more love, more connection, and more sanity, too. In this question are all the answers of family life. If you take nothing else, take this question.

Before you ask it, though, you have to slow down long enough to . . . take . . . a . . . breath. That's it. Just pause. Be still in your mind and your body. And take a big . . . giant . . . breath. Maybe two.

That's the slow.

Now consider an average day or week in your household. Perhaps there is school and work and volunteer time and music lessons and carpool and basketball and meetings and dinner and all the other things that might fill your day.

Is it working?

Does the school you go to feel like a good fit? Is it too far? Do you have to drive farther than you want? Does the drive bring any benefits? Does it feel right? Do you carpool? Do you want to? If you do, is it stressful?

If your child takes a lesson here or is on a team there, does it work for him? For you? For the family as a whole? Does the cost to the family outweigh the benefits to the one? Is it too much? Not enough? Does he get something out of it beyond what he could get elsewhere? Is it temporary or long term? Are you doing it because you want to? Or because you think you should? If it feels like too much—money, time, energy, and so on—is there another way to do it?

If you volunteer at school, if the homework load feels ridiculous, if your weekends are too full, if you are on a committee or board, does it work for you? Do the benefits outweigh the costs? Could the goal be achieved some other way, without the great cost to your family?

The list goes on and on and on. But the simple question remains at the bottom of all of it. Is what we're doing as individuals or as a family working for us as a family? Is there anything we can do to change it? If for some reason we can't change it completely, can we change something about it to make it work for us? (The answer to this by the way is pretty much yes.)

If it's working and bringing you the connection and joy you desire, keep doing what you're doing. If it's not, it's time to figure out how to make a change.

Pause

Late one night, as my teen daughter was trying to fall asleep, she called me into her room to discuss a problem with her schedule—something that was taking a lot of mental space and causing her a lot of worry, especially at this moment, late at night, waiting for sleep to come.

We talked about the issue, what was good, what was hard, and what she hoped the outcome would be. I asked a few questions but mostly tried to listen (not always easy when I want to find answers).

As she began to drift off to sleep, she sighed. I sighed along with her to try to let off some of the steam. "You don't need to come up with the answer right now," I told her.

She sighed again.

"You don't need to do anything at this moment in time except ponder the issue. Just sit in it and the answer will come."

Right then I realized that it is often this small act of pausing that leads us to the big ideas. We can worry and fret and try to force the answer. Or we can tune into the feelings, give the dilemma some space, and find the answer within us.

Sure, we can look outside ourselves for answers, ideas, or inspiration. But more than that, we need to grant ourselves the time and space to sit in the feelings. From there we can more easily figure out what direction to take, what decision to make.

So try this: Next time your children ask to go or do or have something and you find yourself uncertain about the answer, pause. Before you answer, just sit in the question. What's the feeling? Where does the question hit you? Is what they're asking for going to work for you? For the family as a whole?

Next time you're lying in bed fretting about this thing or the other, this decision or another, allow yourself to just sit in the feeling. No need to talk yourself out of it, rather just sigh and let it wash over you without the need for an answer right away.

When we're rushed into an answer there is no time to check in with ourselves. But when we pause and check in with our own needs, feelings, schedules, emotions, we'll find exactly what we need to come to the right answer.

Try this practice for all the questions/dilemmas thrown your way, from Can I sign up for this? to Should I let my child ride her bike to the library? to Should we sell our house? and to everything in between. First pause in the question. Then pause in the feeling. And practice asking yourself, What am I feeling right now?

When we do this, not only are we bringing ourselves closer to the answers but we are also teaching our children to slow down and tune into their own. And what child wouldn't benefit from that lesson?

3

Start the Day with Four Deep, Slow Breaths

The alarm goes off, and you are buzzed into action. Or you snooze. Then it buzzes again, and this time you are really, really on high alert. Time to get up, get dressed, make coffee, make breakfast, get the kids up, pack the lunches, find the shoes, and race out into another day. And all of this runs through your head before your feet even hit the floor.

The habit of being off and running before the day begins is one that can leave us gasping for breath, either figuratively or literally, while leaping ahead into the giant mental abyss of to-dos that is the start of the day. And sometimes it hits us in the middle of the night.

What if, as the alarm goes off, instead of physically and mentally jumping into the never-ending list of tasks, we take a moment to take four . . . deep . . . slow . . . breaths?

Seems cliché, I know, this whole remember-to-breathe thing. But to demonstrate the power of making it intentional, try this exercise. Hold your arm out straight in front of you and point your index finger. Rotate your finger in the tiniest of circles. Now pause. And pay attention to your breathing. What was your breathing doing during that time? If you're like most people, you were probably holding your breath. Not intentionally but just because you were concentrating so hard on what you were doing.

So imagine, if you're holding your breath during this incredibly simple task, what the heck is your breathing doing as you tackle the bigger things? Things like waking kids, cooking breakfast, and making coffee? And then the even bigger things such as going over homework, driving in traffic, and racing against tardy bells?

What if throughout all these processes you did some intentional breathing?

Breathing slowly in.

Breathing slowly out.

Breathing slowly in.

Breathing slowly out.

It slows the body. Wakes us up. Settles the mind. Alleviates anxiety. And slows the heart rate, too.

And what if, instead of our alarm serving as a shocking start to our day, we used it as a reminder to sit up in our bed, plant our feet firmly on the floor, and mindfully take four . . . deep . . . breaths? Before we do anything else.

When I remember to do it I can instantly feel the shift in my day. I can immediately feel the difference in my body. And I am able to absolutely witness a calmer, more connected me. More connected to myself, my husband, my kids, and from that moment on, to the task at hand.

If you need a reminder, put a sticky note on your alarm so that it is the first thing you touch when you reach for the off button. And while you're at it, why not set your alarm for a couple other times of day—just randomly—so you can get onto some serious breathing and calming. After a while it'll just become a part of who you are. Slower, more connected, and most likely a little more joyful, too!

4

Connect the Dots

Several years ago, Carrie Contey and I created a template for a daily writing ritual. It was all about seeing where you've been, where you are right now, and where you want to go in the immediate or distant future. It's a simple tool for focusing on the positive, checking in with your feelings, making your list of to-dos, and setting your sights on some intentions and wishes for future. All done in about five minutes or less.

It's simple but somehow game changing. It can shift your perspective. It can alter your mood. It gives you insights into what you're doing and what you want to do. And it totally lets your mind both focus and wander.

Whatever your current daily ritual, I challenge you to add this exercise and see if you don't love your life a little bit more.

Try it out first thing in the morning as you sit by yourself, incorporate it into your evening time with your partner, or find time somewhere in between.

Sit somewhere comfortable and quiet if you can. Grab a pen and some paper. A dedicated notebook or sketchbook would be perfect. And get ready for your life to change. It really is like a connect the dots for life!

* List seven things you are grateful for right now.

* How are you feeling right this minute?

* What are your intentions for today? (Not your to-dos but your general approach.)

* What did you learn yesterday? (What new insights did you gain?)

* What are your wishes, wants, and desires for the immediate or distant future? (Feel free to fantasize a little. It's fun!)

* What are your to-dos?

5

See Me, Feel Me, Touch Me

Increasing Your Connection

Charles Dickens wrote in *A Tale of Two Cities*, "Eye to eye, voice to voice, hand to hand, heart to heart." And then the Who said on the album *Tommy*: "See me, feel me, touch me, heal me." Even now, in this age of electronic communication, eye to eye, voice to voice, hand to hand, and heart to heart is still the best form of human communication and connection we have.

Try it at home. Try it with your partner. Try it with your kids. See if they don't hear you more and respond better. See if you don't feel calmer and more connected. See if you all don't get what you need just a little bit more.

When you greet each other after being away all day or after a long night's sleep, greet each other eye to eye, voice to voice, hand to hand, and heart to heart. As you approach each other, look into the eyes of your family members and hold that gaze. Give a real hug, and hold it longer than you normally would. As you're going over the day's itinerary, grab a hand and hold it. Speak each other's name as if it were the first time you've ever said it, every single time you reconnect. Or as if you hadn't seen each other in a very long time. Be excited. Pretend at first, and over time I promise it will start to come naturally.

As you talk, touch. As you listen, look. And as you move through the day see if you don't feel more connected to each other and happier too to be together.

It's so simple. And so doable. And so, so powerful, too.

6

Practicing Family Life

Whether it's yoga or exercise or meditation, there are lots of things we do as daily practice. It's what keeps us fit and sane and spiritually energized in order that we may continue on living life the way we want to live it and doing all the other obligatory things that we must do.

What if we made family life a practice, each week having a different area of focus? Like a meditation, like an exercise routine for the heart and mind, family life as practice could bring us exactly the lessons we need and want, and bring us right where we want to be.

We could work on patience one week; giving ourselves a meditation to do each morning and something to practice each day to bring our patience levels to new heights. We could end the day with a reflection, calling to mind all the ways we were patient that day and also the times perhaps we could have done a little more. In the morning we can start again with the knowledge gained and with patience just a little bit more a part of our natural rhythm.

Another week, we could work on love, fully immersing ourselves in living, acting, breathing, and responding with hearts wide open to love. We could make love our guiding force in everything we did with our families. We could wake up thinking a loving thought for each member. We could walk in love all day. And we could end the day reflecting on that love.

That could lead us right into kindness. From there we could practice empathy, making sure to greet our loved ones with a connection to their feelings. Then compassion, understanding, fun, play, humor, and anything else we need to enhance in our family's life together.

Of course we'll slip up. Every good practice has its ups and downs. Of course we'll forget sometimes, too, but the beauty of a daily practice is that we can jump right back in just as easily as we jumped out.

Start today. Start right now, in fact. Start with the thing that is the hardest or start with the thing that is the easiest. Just start. We practice everything else we want to be good at, why not family?

7

Appreciate

In life, especially in family life, appreciations are one of the most valuable tools there is. They are the things I use on a personal level to keep me feeling hopeful, happy, and present with my kids. They are the tools I use to keep my marriage positive. They are the means by which I leap to the other side of crankiness, despair, or hopelessness, and they serve as just the emotional advancement I need to keep me sometimes from losing it altogether. And when I do lose it altogether? Appreciations are the thing that brings me back.

I truly believe that in my personal endeavors, my parenting, and my partnership, appreciations are the key that can unlock the door to a life well lived.

Over the years I have written tutorials on increasing appreciation, even creating a Family Appreciation Banner that can hang in your home as a tool for deeper gratitude and a tool for family connection. I have given workshops on the subject, with parents and kids alike. And I have talked ad infinitum to my children about using appreciations to turn their perspectives around.

Try using appreciations on a daily basis to kick-start your morning or to wrap up your night, as a midday break or an evening meditation.

Right now, write down five things that you appreciate about your family. Maybe write one for each member of your family and one for your family as a whole. And while you're at it, write one for yourself, too.

Feel that? More joy? More connection? More relaxation?

If you take a few minutes each day to focus on appreciating, you will find more to appreciate; what you appreciate appreciates. And your habit may just become contagious.

It helps my kids feel better, too. When they're complaining about life being unfair or how they never get what they want, I ask them to sit down and write five things they appreciate. If they're being really whiny, I might make it ten. Sometimes it takes them awhile, but it almost always has the desired effect.

To spread the love, put two jars, vases, or other vessels in the middle of your kitchen table. Fill one with strips of blank paper and a pen. On the blank strips, write out things you are appreciating throughout the day, for family, yourself, and all the world. Put the written pieces in the other jar. Encourage your family to join in the practice and when the jar is full, read them aloud at mealtime when you are all sitting at the table.

See if it doesn't bump up the love. And see if everyone doesn't appreciate both appreciating and being appreciated.

Picture This

There is a saying that we don't remember things as they are, we remember things as we are. In family life it rings particularly true because each event, each family occasion is viewed by each member, from his or her unique angle, personality, and perspective.

One late fall morning, Kenny and I were lying in bed side by side on a lazy Sunday, talking and staring out the window. As he looked out, he noted that fall was officially over and winter had visibly arrived. I laughed and argued that I didn't think that was true. From where I sat the giant cottonwood that was in the center of my view was noticeably still hanging on to its leaves and looked very much like early fall to me. He scooted over to my side of the bed to see what I was talking about. I scooted over to his side of the bed to see what he was talking about.

We both were right.

Though we sat only inches apart and were looking out the same window, we each saw a different view. And a totally different story.

We can't always see things as others do, but knowing that we each have our own view is the important part. And sharing that view to get the big picture is one of the great advantages of being in a family.

Here's a game you can play to get a glimpse into each other's world. Get out a handful of snapshots from different events in which each member of the family was present. It could be a family vacation or a birthday party or any event at which the whole family was in attendance.

Sit in a circle and give each person one of the photos. Give everyone a few minutes to study the picture. Go around the circle and have each person tell a story about something they remember from that particular day. After everyone has gone, have your family members pass their photo to the person next to them. Then go around again. Go around until everyone has told a story from each photo.

Make sure you allow a lot of time because each story told triggers more and more and more stories, until everyone has a sense that we are all unique pieces of the big picture. Each one bringing something one of a kind.

9

Dropping Love Bombs

A mom I know here in Austin recently shared how her family's "love bombs" totally saved her weekend and beefed up the joy factor for herself and for her whole family. A love bomb consists of a moment to stop and shower her family members with love: words, hugs, squeezes, and a big ol' pile of love. She says, and I quote, "It's impossible for any of us to be unhappy after a love bomb!"

In our family, we have a thing we call Applesauce. It's like a group hug but more animated, and rather than being about the group it's about the person in the center. Someone calls out "Applesauce!!" and we surround one person enveloping him or her with our arms and whole bodies. We then jump up and down in unison, squeezing the loved one tight and chanting, "Applesauce! Applesauce! Applesauce!" It ends with a moment of euphoria for the victim of our love, and for the rest of us, too.

This kind of attention helps when people are feeling malaise or sadness or just a general feeling of not feeling a part of the group. It can be initiated by any person, any time, and if you're feeling especially low you can even call an Applesauce for yourself as in, "Applesauce me!"

The Love Bomb and the Applesauce are total win–win–win; for the recipient, the giver, and for the world at large. And any chance we have to bump up the level of joyful, love-filled celebration, why not?!

Does your family have any random acts of crazy love that you bestow upon each other? Any explosive signs of pure, unadulterated love and affection?

Give it a try. You will be amazed at how incredible it feels to be surrounded by unfettered love. And how connected you will feel as a family when you express yourselves so freely and joyfully.

It is said that giving just five hugs a day and holding each hug for at least five seconds can increase your overall happiness, health, and well-being. So what are you waiting for?

10

Listen with Your Heart Open

I try to listen to my family. Really I do. But I also realize that in my listening I am sometimes distracted or I try to talk too soon or I want them to feel something other than what they're feeling or wanting or needing. I do a little song, dance, or explanation to get them back to happy when they're sad or satisfied when they're mad. Even when they don't want a fix, I offer it. Even when they're really just venting or observing or sharing, I offer solutions. Even when they really just want me to sit there and listen, I talk. "Too many words," says my friend Andrea. Too much noise. Too much input.

I've always been a talker. I even have a certificate from eighth grade that recognized my tendencies: "Most Talkative." So giving up this trait at times is a challenge.

But I'm trying. In fact I have to remind myself on a daily basis to talk less and listen more. And as my kids get older, I see that shutting my mouth is more important than ever. I see that when I listen with my body, mind, and spirit, I get more information, I learn more about their life, I hear more stories, and my family is able to come to their own conclusions sooner about just what needs to be done.

Believe me, I know it's not always easy to listen. Our brains spin with suggestions and ideas and questions. And our bodies want to hurry people along so we can get on with all that needs our attention. But try it. And if you need help pausing your mouth so that your ears and brain can listen, try this.

First take a deep breath. It's always a good start and gives your body the pause it needs so that your brain can follow.

If your child comes to you while you are doing something else, put what you are doing aside. If she is sitting, sit. If she is standing, stand. Put yourself physically with her.

Give her your ear, glance at her on occasion without making her hold your gaze, and let her talk.

Don't fix. Don't judge. Don't assume.

As she finishes up what she's saying, ask her if she is finished. If it is something hard, hug her. If it is something exciting, hug her. If it is something confusing, hug her. Then repeat back in your own words what she said. As you finish, ask her if you got it right.

Before you give input, ask yourself if words are really necessary. If you think they are, then ask your children if they want them. If they do, tell them they can stop you at any time.

Make your input brief and allow enough pauses for them to interject.

Touch a lot. Make sounds of understanding. And end with a lingering heart-to-heart hug.

When our families are struggling, often what they want is comfort, empathy, and understanding, not more words.

And the more we listen, the more room we give them to talk.

11

The Family That Learns Together

A friend of mine, and mother of two growing kids, was experiencing the issue of too many family activities at different times in different parts of town. She was tired of driving here and there to drop one off and pick one up and at the same time trying to fit her own needs in there, too. She wanted to exercise, and she wanted her kids and partner to exercise, too, but she was at her wit's end with scheduling.

Finally she canceled all individual classes for the various ages and instead signed her family up for a karate class for all ages two nights a week.

Two nights a week the karate class was on the calendar, which meant two nights a week that nobody was scheduling anything else. Two nights a week they would meet up at the appointed time all in their gees, all ready to yell, kick, and spend a little time together.

There were definitely some expected benefits. It was physical, which was what they all needed. It eased scheduling, which was what she wanted. It was fun, which was what they all enjoyed. And it was time spent together, which was becoming more and more rare with each passing year.

Another family I know has a daughter on a year-round swim team. Rather than all sign up, which they couldn't do because of their ages, they engaged her to work as the swim trainer, putting her in charge of their training and workout. Once a week they meet for a workout and get instruction from their daughter on proper methods of stroking and breathing.

They are getting their workout and getting time with their teenager too in a way that shifted the dynamics from them simply serving as observers to learning her methods and being with her.

What can you do as a family to increase your time together and be accountable to each other? What can you sign up for that would make you all show up at the same time each week? Could you run together? Play a game? Swim laps? Or just schedule a weekly walk—and stick to it?

Whatever it is, just do it. Together.

12

Slow Sports

For many years, our children were enrolled in our local recreation department's soccer league. It was close to home and fairly laid-back, and the first year seemed easy enough.

The second year, three of our four kids were eligible to play. In three different age groups, they were on three different teams and accordingly, practices were scheduled for five nights of the week. Games were on Saturdays starting at 8 a.m. and continuing until 2 p.m., with breaks in between but not long enough to go home.

Not being all that eager to dedicate our entire schedule to the pursuit of recreational soccer, I approached the league coordinator and asked him if it would be possible to switch things around. I told him we liked to make sure that we had some family time at home during the week. I talked to him about our need for family dinners and homework and downtime together. Though others had warned against asking to change, he arranged the schedules and teams so that we could have soccer and eat our dinner, too, three nights a week. Still not a lot, but better.

The next year, my husband and I arranged to share soccer coaching duties for two of the teams. By volunteering to coach, we could schedule the practices to suit us, making soccer a part of family life, rather than the whole of it. We made soccer a family pursuit as opposed to yet another series of individual obligations. It seemed like a flawless plan.

Two weeks later we were told that the recreation department was paring back and our center would join up with another center across town. This meant driving across town for practice in the evenings. For our family, driving *more* is definitely *not* slow. Especially during rush hour. After much discussion and plotting, we found someone else to coach, and we bowed out of that season's organized soccer altogether.

Just days later, a friend called with an idea. Her husband and kids were interested in playing soccer once a week and wanted to know if we wanted to join them. We would meet at a local park for a weekly game of co-ed, multigenerational soccer.

After just one game, the kids were hooked. They loved the fact that they all got to play on the same team. They loved that the parents played with them, rather than standing on the sidelines shouting out instructions. Kenny loved playing with the kids and with a few other parents. I loved sometimes playing and sometimes visiting on the sidelines. And after practice we could gather for a communal supper until it was time to head home for bed.

This way of playing sports felt like a whole new chapter in our pursuit of slow. Rather than scatter to different teams when we hit the fields, the kids were learning how to work together as siblings and were visibly enjoying the camaraderie it brought. As a parent I loved the collaboration between adults and children.

Through this modeling, the kids could see that the idea of play was a lifelong pursuit, not something reserved merely for childhood and definitely not something that required official uniforms and entry fees. In addition to having time to play, we got a weekly gathering with some of our dearest friends, friends whom we sometimes didn't see for months at a stretch because of being at different schools, on different schedules, and in different parts of town.

Sure, there's a place for organized sports if it works for your family. But in pursuit of slowing down, a family league gave us more than just a game of soccer.

13

Taking Slow Where You Can Get It

As we all know, some weeks are slower than others. Some weeks we are home quite a bit, we are together for long stretches, we eat together, hang out, do homework, and more.

Then there are the other weeks.

The weeks of long workdays, school events, external deadlines, imperative meetings, and social obligations. And in those weeks, when slow can't be about the time but rather about the mind-set, we need to take slow where we can get it.

One such week, I found myself getting home just before bed a few nights in a row. Fortunately, my home support is strong and my husband managed to tend to all the necessary tasks without me. But still, we all needed a little connection, and at the same time my husband needed a break.

Totally fatigued, I lay down in our big bed, clothes on, on top of the blankets. My little one, ready for bed, asked for a story. Sensing that I was too tired to read, my older boy volunteered. The other two joined us in the bed, in various stages of night-time prep.

Before the story began, we did a round of High Point–Low Point, our favorite way of getting in a quick connect and a glimpse into each of our days. Lying in there, facing up to the ceiling, the little one tucked into the middle, we made the rounds, and we all knew a little more about each other than we had just minutes before.

The story then was read by an older child, and all the kids remained until the end. Upon completion, I did my usual meditation while the youngest fell asleep and the other three lay there quietly, thinking about life and the day they had just had.

And that was it. We all went our necessary ways. Some to bed, some to shower, some to finish that last bit of homework.

Total time was less than thirty minutes. But we all felt seen. We all felt heard. And we all felt connected so that bedtime was calm and content rather than frantic and disconnected.

Sometimes we are able to find the connection in even the smallest of moments. That night was a reminder that we need to take slow where we can get it, creating it out of the necessary tasks and allowing it in the smallest of doses.

14

Bedtime Bliss

We all have our bedtime rituals—some utilitarian, some emotional. There is the toothbrushing, face washing, and book selection of course. The backpack readying, the calendar checking, the bedroom floor tidying. There is the mindful calming of the preschooler who tends to amp up at this time of day; like a battery operated toy just before it dies, he needs to be caught before he crashes and burns.

Then, in the big nightly process, with all of our children, at one time or another, there has been that moment, right after the story and right before sleep, when we would have one more tug: we wanting to be done, they wanting to continue. They wanted us for just a minute more—to give us another hug, to have a drink of water, or to have anything to keep us there. Sometimes, too often, one of us would surrender and lie down next to said child for a moment or two only to fall asleep and have that moment turn into a two-hour nap from which we would wake bummed that we had lost our parental evening time.

Then a friend, who is also a mom, introduced us to a whole new bedtime concept. A little experiment she was trying that ended in a total win–win.

This mama friend is someone with whom I have shared many conversations around parenting and mindfulness. This particular time we were discussing the struggles of bedtime. And how with each added child, the process seemed to stretch exponentially and how I often left their bedside feeling drained.

"I'm trying a new thing," she said and my ears perked up. This mama had been doing bedtime for over ten years now. A new thing from her was something to take note of.

At bedtime, after story time, and after lights-out, she tells the children she will stay in the room for her fifteen-minute meditation. As long as they are still and quiet she can do it in there. If they are talking or otherwise interrupting she'll have to take it elsewhere.

Every night is win–win. They calm down until sleep or almost sleep. She gets in her daily meditation, which allows mental clarity, and they get her physical presence. Of course, I had to give it a try.

That first night, I explained the process and how I would stay for fifteen minutes with the timer set. Then at the end, when the timer went off I would get up, walk out, and be done for the night. It not only worked but was brilliant. My son settled in quicker than I have ever witnessed. I got in my meditation, and we ended bedtime feeling connected, slow, and totally at ease. Both of us. By the time I walked out he was just this side of sleep in that blissful eyes-half-closed state. He even gave a little sleepy smile.

It's been nearly a year now since we started this process, and it is pure magic. It's even got my husband doing meditation, which I'm not so sure would have happened otherwise. And we find ourselves looking forward to that post–story time moment instead of dreading the battle that often ensued. While our son is learning a little something about the process and importance of finding your center.

It is about as slow, joyful, and connected as a bedtime process can get.

15

High Point–Low Point

At the end of any big meeting or event, there is the recap. The time when those who were in attendance come together in a smaller, quieter group and go over the details of the day's happenings. It's a time to both acknowledge what worked and ponder what didn't. It's a way too for those in attendance to ponder perhaps how they could have approached something differently then use that information the next time.

In family life we can use this same tool to build greater connection with each other. At bedtime, as everyone is tucked in, brushed, and ready, take a few minutes with each child to tell the story of his day. With little kids you can tell it for them and let them interject where necessary. Go over the events from morning to night with a wide stroking brush, highlighting the pertinent moments such as meeting up with friends at the park or getting a new cubby in school or having a fight with a sibling. You can celebrate the highs and acknowledge the lows, offering them a chance for reflection on how it might be done differently next time.

With bigger kids, let them share the high point and low point of their day. What happened that made them the most joyful, excited, or entertained? And what was the biggest disappointment or challenge? As they finish, you can ask them questions or you can just leave it floating in the air for them to ponder. As they express their struggles, either at home or school, ask them what they felt their part was in it all and how might it be done differently next time.

If you are feeling spacious, share the story of your day as well, also going over the highs and lows and pondering how you might approach it next time if put in the same position.

As each story winds down, end the story with the idea that now we're all going to sleep and tomorrow we get to try it all again. Knowing that at any given moment we all are just doing the best we possibly can—in that given moment.

High Point–Low Point is a great way to wrap it all up in a way that feels super-connected and at the same time leaves us with the idea that every day we can start anew, with new ideas, new approaches, and new chances for living the most connected and joyful life we know how to live.

At the end of the day, what else is there?

16

The Blitz

A Family Tidy Up

I'd be lying if I said that we always find loads of family connection in our housecleaning efforts. I'd be lying too if I said that my children, or their parents for that matter, look forward to doing the necessary household chores. But I really do think we have discovered a way that has made chores decidedly less painful.

When I was growing up, my mom used to hand out chore lists on Saturday mornings, which worked out pretty well because you could choose your own pace for getting things done. We would each get a little piece of paper with our itemized list, according to our age and ability.

The procrastinators could linger in their chores all day long if they want, within reason of course and definitely within that day. And the go-getters in the family could attack their lists and finish up lickety-split.

For the quick pick-me-up however, when it needs to be done *now*, we have come up with another housecleaning method that can really elevate us from the pits, straight into the quite tolerable. And at the same time bring us a little fun and family connection.

We call it the Blitz.

The Blitz isn't for deep cleaning. Rather, it's for those moments just before supper when you look around and realize the house is a disaster. It is also for those weekend mornings when you want to have a leisurely Saturday, but the mess seems prohibitive to feeling truly relaxed. And the Blitz is definitely for those hours just before company arrives at your house. Here's how it works.

First I give a warning that a Blitz is near. I try to give fair warning to allow everyone a few minutes to finish up what they're doing if needed. And I give them a designated time to report to the kitchen.

Once everyone is ready and gathered in one place, we discuss the main points of attack and set the timer for fifteen to twenty minutes, depending on your moods and availability. Once the time starts, it's all hands on deck, everyone moving through the house cleaning, tidying, putting away anything in their path. It helps if you have the music cranked up and a recycling bin and trash bin readily available.

Sometimes we have assigned areas with the understanding that once your area is finished you move into the next or you help someone else. The idea is that you keep moving, productively, until the timer goes off.

Once the timer goes off, that's it. Just finish up the immediate task, and it's over. It's amazing how much can get done in that short amount of time. And it's pretty wild to have everyone flying around the house working at a sort of ridiculously frenzied pace. It's fun. It's funny. And while there are of course the occasional fights, it really does get the job done. For now.

17

Spend Nothing Day

On a normal day, in a usual week, it is hard to go too long without spending money on something. Even if you are not out shopping, consumption manages somehow to creep in, either as a bottle of water or cup of coffee, a quickie snack fix, a random impulse purchase, or some other expenditure not necessarily made as a conscious act. It feels, even in a thrifty family, rather inevitable.

This unconscious spending doesn't necessarily negatively affect the family, but what positive impact could it have on a family if collectively we consciously chose not to spend and to work together on this common goal? Just for one day.

Declare your family's official spend nothing day ahead of

time. Put it on the calendar and make sure it's on a day that can go without spending. You wouldn't want to put it on the same day as the class trip or the company's bowling night.

Just for that one day, agree that as a family you will work collectively to spend nothing. Whether you are all home together on a weekend day or scattered around town at work or school, commit to the idea, both together and individually, to spend absolutely nothing.

See how it feels.

If it's a day you're all together, discuss it throughout the day. How does it feel? Is it hard? Does it take a conscious effort or does it come easily?

If you're apart all day, think about it throughout the day and discuss at day's end. What were the temptations? What were the difficulties? How did it feel to consciously and collectively spend no money?

As you make your way through the world in collective and active pursuit of spending nothing, you not only will be saving a few bucks but will be making a tangible commitment to the family goal and witnessing firsthand just what can be achieved, in the mind and the body, when you commit to a goal and to each other.

Keep a running estimated tally of how much you might have spent, and when you come together at day's end, add up the numbers. Make a family decision about what to do with the money you actively *didn't* spend; for example, you could donate the money to a favorite family nonprofit. Or perhaps you'll put it into a special fund for a special outing or group purchase. Maybe the family will want to invest it in a micro-lending organization so they can see what impact this money can make.

What else could you achieve if you committed to working together? What proverbial mountains could you scale? What difference could you make in the world?

18

One on One

In our household of six, there are lots of words, emotions, and ideas . . . and lots of chaos. While we have lots of time together as a family, getting one-on-one time is definitely a bit more difficult and often requires some planning.

My mom, who raised all nine of us with seemingly very few regrets and a lot of connection, has often said that the one thing she would do differently would be to find a little more time for one on one. Of course, in retrospect it probably sounds easier than it would have been at the time, but still her idea and reminders echo in the raising of my own children.

When she looks back, she realizes that often if she was doing something with one child she tended to have a more-the-merrier kind of attitude. Perhaps because in a life with so much to do, she wanted to make sure to focus on the fun whenever she could, and if some could have fun, why not spread it around?

Now, with my own children, one-on-one time with each child is a monthly goal of mine. One of my favorite scheduled outings is to the grocery store at a "high sampling" time of day. It's fun to walk through with a light list and an empty stomach and to really encourage extreme sampling with one as opposed to trying to keep all four from wreaking havoc on a sample platter.

The goal is just a little face time, and the result is renewed connection and understanding of what's happening in each of my children's worlds. The older they get, the more crucial this feels.

Recently I've come to realize that even if we don't schedule it, I can sometimes steal some mini one-on-one time. I came on this by accident one evening when I realized some videos were due. That same day my son had had a little mishap at school that needed discussing. All the stars aligned for him and me to skip out after supper, and instead of driving or biking the short distance, we walked in order to have time for a conversation.

Slowly we trekked the ten blocks there and back, chatting all the way. I heard about school and friends and a few skateboard tricks he was trying to master. I heard about his struggles with his art teacher and his ideas for his upcoming middle school and in the mere half hour we had together we were able to talk through some issues, unearth some feelings, and come up with a resolution for what had happened that day. Because we were walking it felt easier to talk, and because we were on a necessary errand it felt less contrived than if I had said, "Let's talk about this." And the brevity of it all meant we were barely missed by any of the other members of the household.

We both came back feeling good. We felt more connected, too, and he felt empowered to tackle the issue at school the next day. What it taught me was that the connections I get from one on one can be created any time, any place, as long as I set the intention.

I do this more now, with each of my kids; just steal a few minutes here and there. We can take out the trash, walk to the corner store for milk, clean out the car, whatever. And in that few minutes, we can hash it out, explore ideas, and share a moment, a moment that will keep us going until the next.

19

Deciding to Be Done

Many years ago, my brother drove a cab in Chicago. As he was darting around the city trying to beat the traffic and get a passenger where he needed to go in a timely manner, the guy leaned up from the backseat, touched my brother's shoulder, and said, "Relax. You'll never be first."

Right away my brother relaxed, got the man where he was going, and was even able to enjoy the journey.

I often think of this story as I am buzzing around the house like a hummingbird, tidying, straightening, organizing, doing, doing, doing while life continues all around me. In my head I know we'll never be first. We'll never actually get it all done. We all know that even as you are doing the duties of family life they are already being undone, as you live and breathe.

Sure we can get it tidied, folded, stacked, and stored. We can even clear off all the horizontal spaces, but all the while the kids are growing and at some point we need to stop. Breathe. And take it all in.

We need to stop doing and spend some time just being.

We can take a deep breath. We can sit around and talk. We can let the dishes sit for a bit. We can look at a drawing. We can be the timer for the race or the counter for the pogo stick or the partner for a game of cards.

We can sit outside if we can't bear looking at all that needs tending. Turn our back to the kitchen sink if the dishes on the counter make us shudder. Go for a walk if the sitting goes against our very nature.

It takes a conscious effort to stop. And we certainly can't just stop altogether. But at least a couple of times a day, with each member of the family if you can, or all of them at once if possible, stop for a few minutes and just be. Together.

Enjoy being. The dishes will wait.

Treating Family Time
Like a Good Book

You know that feeling of a good book? When you can't wait to steal time from the day to jump in? When you are somehow able to put everything else on the back burner to immerse yourself in the glorious world of whatever book has got your grip? It's so satisfying, and even decadent in a way, to be able to put the world on hold in pursuit of immersion in a really good read.

One weekend day with book in hand and kids happily immersed in their own work and play, I started thinking. *What if . . .*

What if I could apply that same feeling to family life? What if, when we were home together in the afternoons or evenings, I could give family time that same attention that I give to a really good book? What if, on weekends, we would get stuff done in between the family time, instead of trying to get family time done in between everything else?

Try it. See just how many moments you can steal away from the world and your work, just for a few extra stolen minutes, to be with the best storytellers there are. One person, one day, one lifetime at a time.

Family is the best creative nonfiction there is! And you'll be waiting with bated breath to sink into the next chapter.

21

Syncing Your Calendars (The Old-Fashioned Way)

Some friends of mine—a musician who travels a lot, and his partner—introduced me to the idea of a calendar night. Once in a random while, sometimes weekly, sometimes monthly, sometimes seasonally if need be, they get together, each with their calendar and schedules and pencils in hand.

They go over upcoming shows and events and school affairs for the kids and work schedules and childcare. They fill in the things that are obligatory, they bring their dates together, and they figure out where the voids are, who can fill them, and how to make it work for their family as a whole.

Though nobody in our family travels very much, we do have a lot of people and places and events to keep track of and so we have adopted this idea of a calendar night and adapted it to work for us.

First it was just Kenny and I, figuring out what needed doing and who would do it. We determined where we needed to be and when and how we would get there. We discussed meetings, school events, and other obligatory items that needed a person to attend and a placeholder, too. We evaluated things on a needs basis and determined which could be ditched and which were essential to one or the other or the family as a unit.

We put family nights on there and certain weekend days reserved for hikes or day trips or time spent at home. There were weekly events we wanted to go to: time with friends, a class here or there, time slots in pursuit of favorite hobbies, show times, and so on. We put date nights on there, too, so that our time together wouldn't get forgotten, and we figured out a way to make the weeks as smooth and communicative as possible.

As our kids get older and start to be responsible for their own schedules and tasks, we incorporate them into calendar night as well. There are lessons and babysitting gigs and various other activities that need time and attention from one of us or the other.

Sometimes we forget to give the calendar its proper due, and when that happens the chaos creeps in. With no central information center, we are satellites orbiting each other, and we crash on occasion, as our paths get in each other's way and any chance of connection is fragmented.

"You have a class tonight? But I have a meeting."

"You want me to drive to swim team? But I won't be home until six."

We are attentive to our work calendars full of meetings and deadlines and appointments here and there. When we give the same space to the family calendar and we make intentions for time together as a couple and as a family and even one on one with the kids, life is easier, less overwhelming, more joyful. And definitely more connected, too.

So if you're feeling overwhelmed by the current state of activities, take a look at your calendar. Call a family meeting to discuss everyone's events and obligations. Figure out what is crucial, what brings joy, what can be done to create slow, joyful connection in the process. Who might get time alone with one parent or another? Who might enjoy a solo ride with Mom? Or an evening home alone with Dad? And how can we make sure we truly see and enjoy each other in the midst of this busy time?

22

Go Outside and Play

When I was growing up, *Go outside and play* was a sentence I heard all the time. It came in all forms, from excitement about a beautiful day to my mother's exhaustion at having us all inside for too long.

Going outside seemed easy then, with so many kids on the block to choose from and so much space to run around. The big kids watched the little kids, and the little kids just did what they were told. Mostly.

Today I use that same sentence quite often as I tell my kids, "Go outside and play!" There is the feeling that to not go outside would be a waste of a beautiful day. Or sometimes the feeling that if people don't get out of the house and get off the screens and move their bodies and engage in physical play *now*, someone is going to freak out.

I have talked to lots of parents about this same thing. They remember being told often to go outside and play as kids. They try it now, and it doesn't always work. There aren't as many kids around, there isn't always the same freedom to roam, and the attractions of the indoors are just more than they used to be.

When I want my kids to go outside, it's because I want them to experience something other than the virtual. I want them to swing, climb a tree, roll in the grass, play hide-and-seek, or even lie on a blanket under a big blue sky. I want them to feel the natural world. I want them to get out of the confines of the house and explore. Even if that exploration means fighting over who's it.

Admittedly, oftentimes they resist the transition from inside to outside. Even on the most beautiful day. Even when they have been cooped up for hours or days. Actually, *especially* when they have been cooped up for hours or days. Or when they take hours on a weekend morning going from bed to breakfast to a non-pajama'd state.

And yet, when they do finally make it out there, they are happier. They get along better. And, at the risk of sounding totally cliché, they feel more alive.

Now I have a surefire way to get them outside without an argument. I go out there first. I go out without making a big deal about it. I walk quietly out the door and start piddling about the yard. I water plants or pick up bikes and skateboards. I pick a few weeds and arrange the outdoor furniture. I wander about for not very long at all and then, lo and behold, out they come one by one. It's another win–win and, quite literally, a breath of fresh air. And then I can even sneak back in, if need be, leaving them out there to play.

23

Camp Out at Home

We were nearing the time for winter break and were starting to feel the drudgery of our daily routine.

One sunny Sunday, my daughter had a friend over, and they asked for the tent to be set up in the yard for them to play in. They wanted some privacy and an escape from the interfering eyes of the rest of the family. We set it up, they played in it all day, and when playtime was over, we left it up.

That night, two of my kids asked if they could sleep out there. I argued that it was a school night and that just wasn't going to work and *blah, blah, blah*. They argued back that it would work and it would be fun and they would go to bed earlier if they were allowed to sleep in the tent. I realized that when we camp, the kids *do* actually go to bed earlier than usual because they are guided more by the sun than the clock, so I agreed—with the condition that if it got too nutty I could pull the plug at any time.

They settled in to the tent with sleeping bags, flashlights, and books and were indeed asleep earlier and easier than if they had gone to bed inside. The next morning I made a little fire in the fire pit in the yard before I woke them. As I called their names they popped right up, excited about their unusual school day location.

As they got dressed in the tent I brought their breakfast outside and they ate by the fire in the chilly morning air. They were ready to depart a good fifteen minutes earlier than usual, and they rode to school excited to tell their friends about their backyard campout.

The next four nights we repeated the drill. Bedtimes were simple. Wake-up times were a dream. And the general malaise that was threatening to overtake the family as we neared our well-deserved school break was overcome. We coasted into winter break rejuvenated, renewed, and ready for whatever we needed to do.

I realize that not everyone can pitch a tent in the yard or serve breakfast around a fire. But when the routine is feeling like too much drudgery, we can all do something to shake things up. We can sleep on the family room floor, switch rooms, eat breakfast on a picnic blanket under the dining room table, and otherwise change the way it's always done.

Whatever you can do to alter your reality, do it. I guarantee that it will get you through to the next phase, happier, revitalized, and more connected, too.

Slow Summer Camp

Summer is a great time for kids. School is out, the pool is open, and the hours, full of possibilities, stretch out before them. Unfortunately, these same hours stretching out before them sometimes run in direct competition with parents' need to work or a kid's need to be entertained.

For some families, summer camp is easy. They know where they want to go, and they have the means to get there. For others, though, money can be tight, and the kids end up at a camp that might be less than desirable. For still others, it feels luxurious, especially if one parent is staying at home.

Either way, this slow summer camp idea, which I learned from a friend, is a perfect way to send your kids to camp without the cost—with the added connection of spending fun time together.

She and three other families have created something they call Camp Co-op. It is a four-day-a-week camp that in some ways harkens back to the summer of my own youth, when the days were structured around hanging out outside, doing fun stuff, and playing with friends.

The four families are each responsible for the camp one day a week. The parent in charge for the day can create a camp-like activity for the kids either at home or somewhere out in the community, and the total cost is up to each parent. They either find something free to do, like a craft, a project, or a visit to a nearby swimming hole, or they can choose something grander like an amusement park, museum, or a movie.

In just one standard week of camp, the kids roller-skated, swam in a creek, and biked downtown. In the ensuing weeks, they sewed, bowled, swam, explored the capital, and had more fun than they could have ever had on their own or in a regular camp.

Slow Summer Camp, Camp Co-op, whatever you want to call it. It's summer camp. It's family connection. It's exploration of your hometown. It can be free. It's fun. And it's sort of getting to have your cake and eat it, too.

Who doesn't want a piece of that?

Community Service, Family Style

To connect as a family within the home is of course one of the main goals of Slow Family Living. Seeing each other for who you are and valuing each individual within the family dynamic is a key part of the process of slowing things down.

To volunteer as a family and take that feeling of connection out into the world is not only a gift to the greater community but can be a huge gift to your family as well. It will give you all an understanding of how you rely on each other, how you interact, and how you can work together for the greater good.

When you step out into the world as a unit, with the goal of sharing your family's gifts and talents, the connection you all feel to each other will be expanded beyond belief. And the connection you feel to the world around you will grow exponentially—each and every time you do it.

Before you jump in, as a family, figure out what will help you find a good fit for your family. What things are important to you? What do you like to do? Where do you often go? Which groups do you support? What causes interest you? What school, church, nature, or community groups are you members of? If you can't quite figure out where you fit into the community, ask yourself what things you like to do, as individuals or as a family. What hobbies do you have? What passions do you pursue? What segments of the community spark your interest or curiosity?

Whether you are a long-time resident of a town or brand-new still unpacking, what talents and gifts can you bring to the table that will at once help you celebrate your family and simultaneously enhance your community?

Our own volunteer time has changed over the years, depending on our current interests or state in life. We have sat on the curb and collected shoes for refugees. We have cleaned up creeks, delivered newsletters for a cause, served at school events, dispensed food and clothing, and worked on a smaller, individual scale, providing help to a specific family.

For the most part, our volunteer time in the community feels good for us all. It might be difficult sometimes to put ourselves out there, especially for the older kids who might be nervous or embarrassed or just uncertain about their role. Mostly though, especially after we've gotten started, it's fun to present ourselves as an entity to the community and to feel connected to something bigger than just ourselves.

No matter how old your children are or how many are in your family, you can find a cause, a niche, a place in the community that needs tending, and tend it as a family.

You will not only be serving the community but you will be seeing each other in a whole new light, as a unit stepping out into the world. The connection and joy you will feel and share will be beyond measure.

And if you're looking for another way to volunteer your time and talents, consider volunteering in your child's classroom. At the risk of sounding like an infomercial, in as little as thirty minutes a week, you'll increase connection, meet his classmates, learn more about your child's life, and enhance the classroom experience, not just for your son or daughter but for every child in the room.

26

Magnetic Attraction

A Slow Walk with a Purpose

When the kids are small, there's nothing simpler than a good old-fashioned family walk. Just pop the wee ones in the stroller and hit the streets, wandering the neighborhood or aimlessly roaming a local park, taking in all the world has to offer as you saunter by.

As the kids get older, though, it can be harder to convince them that a family walk will be fun and relaxing (though, of course, it will).

So how can you get everyone on board with the idea?

My husband does carpentry, and one of his tools of the trade has proven a great walking tool: a giant magnet on a stick. It is a powerful device that is used at the end of the day to clean up the job site and make sure there are no errant nails, screws, or metal shards lying around. And it turns out to be a fun activity for the kids as we're on an evening walk, taking turns searching for metal detritus of all sorts on the sidewalks of our neighborhood.

Back home, we sit in the yard examining our finds. We wonder aloud what some of the items are and how they got where they were. We concoct stories and reflect on what we've found together.

You don't need a giant magnet to connect with each other on a family walk of your own. Bust out the hula hoops, play hopscotch, take out an old camera—just spend a little extra time together making the ordinary extraordinary. Get out of your rut, break the usual patterns, throw a little pointless fun into the time you spend together. It'll be what they remember. I swear. Even if you do it only once.

27

Do-Over

Sometimes it happens. The snappy retort, the snarky request, the cranky comeback, or the overall nasty tone with no tangible explanation. We all do it. And the real danger comes when it takes on a life of its own, spiraling out of control until we're all caught up in it.

We all know it can happen. The question is how to stop it before it takes over.

Enter the Do-Over, a technique I learned from my sister-in-law, an amazing elementary guidance counselor. It's a simple tool we can all use to make sure that family life stays joyful and foul moods don't get too out of control.

Say your child asks you what's for supper as you stand over the stove. It's an innocent enough request, but in your haste you snap and say something like, "Split pea soup, if I can get some help around here."

You catch yourself.

And you call for a do-over.

Right there on the spot, you cry, "*Do-over!*" And your child knows to ask the question again. Only this time you reply, "Split pea soup, and it'll be ready soon. Think you could help me get the table ready for supper?"

Say you ask your child to take out the garbage. She flips and answers in a cranky way, "Why are you always asking me? I'm doing something."

"Do-over," you say, as calm as can be. You ask the question again. This time she replies, "I'll do it in a few minutes. I just want to finish this chapter."

Even our five-year-old has mastered the do-over. He'll say something snarky and catch himself. "Wait, let me do that again." And he'll restate his question in a kinder, gentler tone.

The do-over not only brings more joy and more connection, but it can keep one little harsh reaction from infecting an entire afternoon.

Long live the do-over!

28

Happy You Day!

As a culture, we celebrate Mother's Day, Father's Day, even Grandparents Day. In a little town in New Jersey there is even a Children's Day, and the town has been celebrating it for well over a hundred years. It is a weekend-long event full of parades and festivities and costumes and games and old-fashioned pageantry and a celebration of all things childlike.

In our house we have established our own kind of children's day. Admittedly, we don't have parades or floats or costumes, but we do celebrate each individual child—one at a time.

It started one day a few years back, when the kids were feeling like a little special treatment was in order. Life was just getting too monotonous and feeling a little mundane. And so we declared that we would hold our first children's day, celebrating one child at a time, starting with the first name selected randomly from a hat.

The rules were simple. On the child's appointed day, which would then be named for them, they would get special treatment all day plus a one-on-one walk with Mom or Dad to the bakery around the corner where they could select their favorite item.

Everyone in the family was excited for the first children's day to begin.

On that first day, the kids jumped in completely. They made each other's beds. They picked up each other's dirty clothes off the floor without commentary. They wrote little notes to each other and put them under pillows. They gave each other little gifts, regardless of whose special day it was.

Because each one knew their day would come, there were no cries of "Unfair" or "He always gets to go to the bakery!" Instead, as we walked out of the door, there were cheers of "Have fun! See you later!"

The feeling of kindness and love was palpable. And it spread over into the days before and after, too. The celebrated child felt honored, loved, and appreciated. And the celebrators felt excited, happy, loving, and helpful.

It is the ultimate win–win.

29

Make 'Em Laugh

Take a minute to think about the hardest parts of your family's day.

What times are continuously crazy making? Is it morning? Dinner? Bedtime?

What are the habits? Who does what over and over? How do you react? How do your children react?

In a word, sum up how you feel at these times.

How do you *want* to feel?

Now think of one thing you do that makes you laugh uncontrollably. Is it a ridiculous face? A crazy sound? A wrestling match? Or maybe standing on your head?

The next time you have to engage in that obligation that makes your family so crazy, start instead with this ridiculously silly thing. Stand on your head next to your child's bed as you wake him for school. Before bedtime, engage him in a ridiculous face contest. At the dinner table, instead of telling him he needs to eat, announce in an excited voice that it would be so cool if, after everyone finished eating, they would be up for a wrestling match in the living room.

Instead of repeating our patterns of resist and desist, why not turn it around with a little playful fun?

They'll feel better. You'll feel better. It's another win–win for family life.

Say Good-Bye Like
You Mean It

What if, every once in a while, we bid our partners farewell and said good night to our children as if it were the last time we'd see them for months on end?

What if, every now and again, we crawled into our child's bed with her at bedtime and lingered for a minute and gave her a full-on hug, while we squeezed her little face and gave her big, loud kisses and heartfelt wishes for the sweetest dreams possible?

What if, every once in a while, as our partner was walking out the door on his way to work, we put down the electric bill or cell phone or dirty dishes and walked out the door with him all the way to the curb and then gave him a backbreaking love squeeze that lasted for minutes on end? What if, as he was taking that first step away, we put down everything in our hands and minds and made out with him as if we were teenagers saying good-bye at the airport?

Not all the time, mind you. That might get annoying.

But every now and again?

What if?

31

Ponder Invitations
(And Practice Saying No!)

If you have school-age children, invitations to parties and events come in at a regular and sometimes rapid-fire pace from every direction. Some weekends might be filled with two, three, or even four invitations to birthday parties, special events, and more.

Before you respond, put the invitation aside, pause, and ponder. In this day of electronic communication, we sometimes feel obliged to respond right away as if there were some urgency. As you ponder, ask yourself simply, Do I really want to go? Does my child really want to go? What else is going on that week? How will it impact the whole family? Do I need to build in some time just to (inhale) be (exhale) together?

When we receive invitations, we feel flattered and also feel some strange societal obligation to attend. Ask yourself, though, what is needed more: A party? Some concentrated family time? A busy happy party? An uninterrupted weekend at home? Only by pausing and asking can you discover the true answer.

In our house, the idea of not attending a party was at first met with scorn by the kids. "What? We're not going? But we were invited!" However, as Kenny and I made the process of invitations more mindful, the parties we did attend felt more satisfying, and we strengthened our ability to see when it was time to extend outward or pull inward, either as individuals or as a family unit.

The answer of whether to accept or decline changes from week to week, and from party to party, but the goal of creating satisfying, connected weekends, wherein we all try to get what we need to feel more sane, more relaxed, more joyful, and more connected going into the next week, definitely remains the same.

32

Playing Hooky, Family Style

Sometimes, every now and again, we just need a break.

In the work world, it's called a personal day. In the school world, it's called hooky. And in family life, we call it a random necessity. It's to be used in those emergency times when daily life feels like it's getting too hard or too cranky. When it feels like there is too much in-house fighting, too much fatigue, and too much disconnection.

In our house, we call it Slow Family Hooky. For it to work smoothly, it needs to be planned well and planned ahead of time, but not *too* far ahead of time. Because a family has so many variables in a daily schedule, it's best planned together and with a calendar spread out before you, picking a day that will work for everyone.

Several nights beforehand we put all our ideas for activities on the table. We could go for a hike in a favorite park or take a day trip somewhere we've longed to go. We could stay home to do a project or even just spend the day reading. Mostly, though, our hooky days are spent outside, enjoying a true getaway from the daily routine.

At school the next day, when the absent slip asks us the cause for our absence, we simply write "Family matter." Which is the truth, the whole truth, and nothing but the truth!

And we all return to the world feeling ready once more to take on the daily grind.

33

Family Homework

As a family we have tried a variety of schooling in search of the method that worked best for each child and for us as a family. We have homeschooled, gone to charter schools, private schools, and to our neighborhood public school.

All had their high points. And all had their lows. Each one had elements that really worked for each child and for our family as a whole, and some that didn't. Each time, in each school, with each teacher, we tweaked what we could, changed what we were able, or tried something else.

We landed, finally, at a nearby public school, one mile from home and close enough to bike. It is a great community with some amazing teachers, but for us as a family, and for us philosophically, one of the major issues was homework; too much of it. In the lower grades it was manageable enough. We sought out teachers that were tolerable of a little slacking or at least understanding of the fact that occasionally fatigue, extra activities, or family life might take precedence.

One year we were lucky to have a teacher who followed Alfie Kohn's lead and assigned no nightly homework other than reading. She believed after school for second graders should be full of play and family time. Instead of nightly homework, she assigned monthly family projects. These were fun activities around a certain subject or topic, and the idea was that they were to be done as a family over the course of an entire month. Parental involvement was absolutely encouraged, as was sibling involvement or even Grandma if she happened to be nearby.

We all loved these projects and looked forward to them each month. They were thoughtful, fun, creative, educational, and wide open for familial interpretation. These projects brought a great amount of connection to our family as we tackled each one. They were cause for many amazing outings that were chockfull of exploration and discovery.

It gave us a glimpse into the idea of homework creating connection instead of fighting. Rather than a lone child hunched over a paper working on endless problems, we could truly do it collaboratively, either as a group or one-on-one.

From that point on, the pressure of homework was lifted. Not just in that class but for all of our children as we applied the family projects idea to everything, and we made the process our own.

If a kid was too tired, we did it with him. We would discuss each problem and make sure he understood the concept, and we would serve as the scribe to his dictation. We realized the purpose of homework was not mindless filling in of the blanks but an understanding of the concepts; and if this was the point, what difference did it make how it got done. We could write or recite. We could edit while they read aloud. We could color, draw, write, and do it together with our eyes on the prize of learning rather than work completed alone. And recognize that all of life is a collaborative process full of brainstorming and help. Why not let school be the same?

34

Keeping a Family Journal

Lots of us make baby books. Or at least lots of us start them.

What if, instead of a book for each child, we had a family journal? What if, instead of stats and facts, we had a book where we could write of family adventures or happenings? Of auspicious occasions or events? Or even of silly phrases and words uttered by our children? Or sentimental journeys taken by us as parents?

There's lots of ways to do it. And it's never too late to begin; even if you've been on this parenting journey for a while now, you can start with a tiny memoir of where you've already been or start with right now. Here. Today.

Because this book will serve your family right through until your children are grown, you'll want to get something solid, substantial, and maybe even something flexible as well where you can add more pages or insert photos or more.

A three-ring binder will serve perfectly. Or a spiral sketchbook with heavy-duty paper. Or a scrapbook that you can write in, glue in, draw in, and more.

You can separate it into categories such as family quotes, vacations, milestones, and birthdays. Write short anecdotes or encounters. Write of birthday celebrations. Write funny things your kids say. Things you hear yourself say that you never thought you would utter.

Decorate the cover with a family motto or a family picture as you are right now or a collage or painting or whatever suits your family best. Punch holes in folders with pockets or manila envelopes. Insert photo pages or just use card stock with photo corners.

Don't feel pressured to write lengthy prose or essays. Unless you want to.

Don't feel compelled to make it perfect. Unless you're into that kind of thing.

Don't think you have to post everything. Unless you might want that info down the road.

Just post what you can. When you can. However you can.

Write down the first time someone sat up. How you felt on the first day of kindergarten. Where you went on a family road trip. Or any other information you feel is pertinent to your family life.

And if you forget to add something, add it later or just move on.

Ten years from now, twenty years from now, you'll be glad to have it.

And your kids will be glad, too.

35

Spacious Transitions

Transitions from one activity to another can cause chaos or crankiness in family life, to put it mildly. Whether dealing with small children, teens, or admittedly even our partners, freakouts can occur when transitions of the group are made. There is a feeling of rushing or being rushed, or just feeling overwhelmed by the move from one thing to the next.

By child number four, Kenny and I have finally figured out that when going anywhere with small kids, the bigger the window, the happier the travels. When the toddler's exclamations of "I do it" send one of us into a tailspin, we know we haven't allowed enough time for moving from one thing to the next. When I am leaning over the computer for one last email check before I head out, I know I am possibly creating more chaos than it's worth. Later, if we can't pause for a second to examine a tiny rock, pointed out to us on the sidewalk and shining perfectly in the sun, we know we've made things too tight. For just five more minutes added to our window, we could connect, foster imaginations, and make our kids believe that, yes, life is indeed about stopping to examine the things that glitter on the sidewalk in the sun.

Whether we are rising in the morning, settling in the evening, or heading somewhere in between, the transitions can be tough. To slow things down mentally and physically, factoring in just minutes more for the move from one thing to the next can help ease everyone, mind, body, and spirit.

Try setting the alarm a few minutes earlier. Five more minutes of sleep isn't going to change things, but five or ten more minutes of time in the morning to breathe, to prepare, and to wake up the family can definitely ease morning transitions.

Get into the habit of preparing for transitions ahead of time whenever you can and then enjoy the minutes of waiting. We often put off the approach or start of things until the last possible minute. This applies to dinner prep, school pickup, appointments, and more. Five more minutes of email or work time isn't going to make a significant difference in your career, so put it down for another time and get a mini jump start on meals or homework or bedtime. Eliminating last-minute startups will also eliminate last-minute panic.

When there is more time for transitions, there can be more relaxation on everyone's part. And we won't freak out if our child wants to pause for a second to examine some shimmery object. Who knows, it could be just the pot of gold we've been seeking.

36

Just Ten Extra Minutes

I was driving across town the other day on my way to a meeting. Before that I had dropped my oldest daughter off at a class and gone to the bank and the post office. Before that I had been at home with my husband as we discussed the day's events and who needed to do what, when, and where. Before that he had gotten our middle two up and out to school, made breakfast, put beans up to soak for dinner, and put dough ingredients in the bread maker for lunch.

It was kind of a usual morning really—full of all the moments that make up a rather typical family morning. Breakfast, backpacks, papers, errands, drop-offs, and still more thought of more meals.

It felt calmer than usual though. It felt easy and friendly and free from any arguments—the kind of arguments that can admittedly find their way into our typical family morning. There were none of the panicky moments around finding the backpack or socks, locating bike helmets, finding car keys, or even making food.

Everyone was chill. Everyone was doing what they needed to do. And everyone got out the door and got to their respective right place at the right time.

As I drove to the meeting, with more than ample time to get where I was going, I sat in the parking lot and made a necessary phone call in the extra few minutes I had. I pondered, what made the difference. And I realized that really the entire difference was about ten minutes extra of time in the morning. And that extra ten minutes set us all free from panicking, fighting, and fretting about all that needed to get done.

That morning at wake up, rather than waiting for second call which comes ten minutes after first call, the kids got out of bed. They then had ten minutes extra to do all their stuff, which meant that when they couldn't find their backpack, we had ample time to find it. When they dawdled getting socks, we had time to sit and sip our coffee and let them dawdle without fear. When they took their sweet time getting out the door and into their bike helmets, we too could take our sweet time and we could take a minute to breathe, while we waited.

At the post office, I didn't care that there were a few people in line ahead of me. At the bank I happily pulled up behind the car in the drive-through and while I waited, I enjoyed the minute to read a text. As I drove to my meeting, I could take it easy, let people merge in front of me, and enjoy the ride instead of feeling the angst of possibly being late or just barely on time.

Ten minutes.

We don't need to revamp our lifestyle from top to bottom to feel more relaxed, more joyful, more connected. We just need to add in ten extra minutes.

Hard at first, but easier in the long run.

37

This I Believe

For many years, there was a radio show on public radio called *This I Believe*. It was a beautiful feature in which people from all walks of life would share, in simple terms, one of their basic beliefs. Listening to it, I often found myself crying, or pondering some deep thought or new idea, or being called to action to some great cause. It was powerful stuff.

We've adapted the idea into a family exercise. Sit in a circle, around the table perhaps, and start with the saying, "This I believe . . ." For example, This I believe . . . that our family loves to go on hikes. This I believe . . . it's been way too long since we took a family vacation. This I believe . . . our family eats a lot of popcorn. This I believe . . . our family is in a better mood when we eat dinner together.

If you like, think bigger. What are the values you hold dear and try to live by? Which ones would you like to exercise more as a family? Community? Leadership? Authenticity? Spontaneity? Write down your answers and revisit them together.

This is a fun exercise and a good glimpse into seeing what everyone in your family holds as truth.

38

Throw the Rules Out the Window

When I was a kid, we had pretty strict bedtimes, but one night a year, we were given carte blanche and we had Stay Up As Late As You Want Night. It was a big deal for everyone and was talked about and planned out weeks and weeks ahead of time. We had treats ready and games prepared and my mom made sure the anticipation was as fun as the night itself.

We're all still talking about it today. More than forty years later!

So if you want to surprise your children and give them something they'll remember for a lifetime, every now and again, throw the rules out the window.

If you want to milk it a little, plan it out ahead of time and let the kids in on the planning. But if you're feeling spontaneous and thinking your family needs a little injection of excitement, do it on the spur of the moment. Just like that, no rules!

The impact will be greater, the less you do it, so for their sake, and your own sanity, do it sparingly.

Of course it will vary from house to house, as do the rules and restrictions, but here's a few examples just to get you going . . .

Instead of dinner at the table, have a picnic in the living room.

Serve breakfast in bed on a school morning.

Let the kids sleep in their clothes.

Read in bed as late as you want.

Let their bedroom get messy.

Eat cereal for supper.

Watch TV while you eat.

Leave your toys out after a game.

Serve ice cream for breakfast.

Sleep in a sleeping bag on the floor

Have fun! And get creative.

39

Timed Talking

We all have days with our families that are, well, to put it nicely, less than stellar. There are days that are full of teasing and picking on each other and harsh tones and nobody listening to anyone and some pretty incredible snarkiness in just about every direction. I blow my top. My husband blows his. The kids blow theirs until we're all pretty much spent.

Enter Timed Talking—a way for everyone to say their piece in peace.

We call everyone together and we sit in a circle either around the living room or kitchen table or outside. We set the timer for five minutes, and we begin. The only real rule is that when someone is talking, the rest of us listen without distraction or interruption. The speaker chooses the topic and is free to digress or not.

Often the talk is about what the infractions were that were witnessed and felt and made. Or about how one felt before, during, and after the crankiness began, and what we could have done differently. Until, ding! The timer goes off and it's the next speaker's turn. And around the circle we go.

Timed talking lets the storm pass so we can move on into a beautiful new next and a deeper and more understanding connection to each other.

What Do You Need?

I often suggest that families post a What Do You Need? chart. The template is simple: a whiteboard, chalkboard, bulletin board, or even a piece of paper posted on the fridge or some-where visible to one and all. On the board put a space for each person in the household, a space for the family as a whole, and a separate space for the household. Across the top, write: "What Do You Need?" Invite all family members to fill in their own space with things they need: a warm shower, renewed driver's license, folded laundry, dark chocolate, time alone, time to-gether, a walk, a run, or whatever.

Having the board up and accessible means that when you think of the thing you need, you can add it to the chart for all to see. Not only does it serve as a great reminder for the person in need but it's also a great way to have others help you make sure your needs are met. In a growing household, it allows each family member to more easily and cooperatively move toward getting their needs met *and* meeting the needs of others. Isn't that what family is all about?

It's amazing how good it feels to put things on your own list and to be able to see others' lists and help others move toward getting their needs met—short term and long term—and then to cross items off accordingly. And if you've ever wanted a feel-good family moment, imagine an eight-year-old studying the chart and saying, "Oh, Mom, don't forget. You and Papa need to have a date." I was certainly glad he added that one to my list!

I highly recommend you give it a try in your house. Whether you need an ice cream cone or a weekend at a spa, a new pair of shoes or a new method for clearing the table, put it out there and see what comes your way.

Fantasy Island

While we can't always get what we want, and we can't always grant our kids their every desire, it's fun to dream a little.

So in our house we make it into a game . . .

We sit at the table and play a game called What Do You Want?, like it's a game of Ping-Pong. Only instead of two players and a ball, it's got six players and a lot of big ideas.

One person starts simply by stating something they want. It can be a thing (like a new pair of binoculars) or an experience (like a trip to Mexico) or a concept (like more time home alone or a room of their own). Around and around we go in no particular order, just shouting out ideas one at a time. While all those around the table exalt at the desires stated, "Oh yes!

Awesome! PERFECT!" And maybe even join in the want, "Oooh! I want that, too!"

We aren't granting any magic wishes. We aren't keeping any lists. But we are all getting to feel the satisfaction of stating out loud the things we want without anyone at all saying no. We walk away from the table when all the ideas have been exhausted and everyone feels satisfied with their list now out there for the universe to maybe get a hold of. It's all accepted. It's all exciting. And in that shared moment of time it all feels like total possibility.

Now that we all know what we want, we feel that much closer to getting it, and closer to each other, too.

Sigh. Forgive. Let Go. Move On.

Squabbles are an inevitable part of family life. To maintain the lifelong connection that we all so desire, we've got to . . . Sigh. Forgive. Let go. Move on.

And if we want to make sure the hurt doesn't fester and grow, we need to . . . Sigh. Forgive. Let go. Move on.

I learned this from my own mom, eighty-seven as of this writing, our familial matriarch and a trusted friend to hundreds. She taught me this skill as a child though of course when I first learned it, I didn't quite understand its magnitude. Now, as an adult, as a longtime partner to Kenny, as a mother of four, as a sibling to eight, and as an in-law to lots and friend to many, it is evident to me just how crucial it is to master this skill. How vital it is to . . . Sigh. Forgive. Let go. Move on.

The sigh is essential. It serves as a physical expression of the hurt and a tangible way to let go. It is an inhale, big and deep, and an audible exhale that holds the release we so powerfully need.

The forgiveness is next. It must be real, and it must come from a place of love.

Then we can let go. Seriously. Let go. That's it. Face your palms to the sky for a physical reminder. Let go of the pain and aggravation and let go of that moment of fighting that seemed so intense.

Now move on. To the next minute. And the next, and the next. Peacefully moving forward to together moment by moment into a lifetime.

43

Make Stuff Together

As a mom and as a partner, I believe that sometimes, coming together around a project can bring us the family connection that we all need.

Whether you are sitting together at the table working on a drawing or in the kitchen whipping up a feast or in the garage crafting a little birdhouse, the task of making things together can really bring a family together.

I wrote a whole book about making stuff together. It's called, cleverly enough, *Make Stuff Together*. I cowrote it with my good friend and mothering confidante Kathie Sever. We have made lots of things together, with and without our children, and we both agree that creating something together can bring family life to a deeper place, sparking unexpected conversation, trust, and joy.

So whip out the cookbooks, the craft books, the woodshop books, or just some paper and crayons: the family that makes stuff together can find joy and connection in the process and in the finished project as well.

Make a family flag celebrating your connection to each other. Write a song or poem about your family. Get dressed up and take a family portrait or make a movie together. Invent a special family dessert.

Recently, we created a symbol for our front door, an image that would serve as a reminder to all who entered our home—including ourselves—that a family lived here; a family focused on joy and love and connection and, we hope, peace and kindness, too.

The symbol is an aluminum star into which the word *Peace* is stamped in plain, bold letters, to which we've added the word *Patience*.

The star is our reminder that we can leave all that mess and worry out there. If we are lucky we can bring in the calm that we all need and love and desire, too. Or we can bring the tears that we need to let flow. Or the utter exhaustion that we couldn't face until that very minute. Or the problem that we can't deal with alone.

What can you create together as a family?

Dinner Co-op

In our house, we try for family dinner most nights of the week. Regardless of the food, we love the connection of facing each other, sharing a meal, and sharing our highs and low of the day. Even when it's not pure bliss as parents we like the feeling of all of us together.

We try to focus on the process of the sitting down together instead of worrying about what that meal will be. But really, a good meal bumps it up a notch, without a doubt. And I definitely give my husband kudos for being able to whip something out of nothing and make it pretty appetizing, too. But we all know, there isn't always time, or food in the fridge, or energy, after a day of work, errands, school, homework, all of the above, and then some.

Enter the Family Dinner Co-op.

Friends of ours have participated in ever-evolving dinner co-ops over the years—some started and stopped, while others went on for years with the same three or four families participating.

Whatever way you decide to go, however you arrange it, the Family Dinner Co-op will definitely let you enjoy the family dinner more, find more connection, and enjoy the process— without always having to be the one to get the good food on the table.

You can structure it however you like, but there are definitely some things to keep in mind as you plan. Proximity is one. Similar size families helps, too. And if you're a gluten-free or vegetarian or omnivorous eater, it helps to find others who are on the same page or at least willing to try.

First, find a few families you know within the parameters that meet your needs. Of course you can find others too but the easier it is, the longer it will continue. Find those families that you see every day in your travels—maybe you're at the same school, perhaps you work in the same office, or perhaps you even live on the same block.

Once you gather the necessary families, plan a little kick-off potluck at a park or at a house or somewhere you can all sit together. Next create your schedule of making meals. Each of the families will take turns making meals during the week for the other families so picking a night that suits your family will promote the co-op's longevity.

On your given night, you make dinner for each of the other families. In the various groups I've seen, three families seems to be the magic for co-op sustainability. And cooking for three families is within most people's abilities whereas more than that can sometimes get a little tricky or a little complicated.

On the other two nights, dinner is delivered to your door. Ready to serve or just heat and eat. With dinner co-op, you have family dinner planned three nights a week. The fourth night it's leftovers and then there's still plenty of time for popcorn, cereal, and smoothies!

You could also plan one night a month or a season to have dinner together as a group, creating even more together time.

The Family That Cooks
Together

For many years I was the main cook in the house and as my firstborn got old enough to reach the counter she joined me in my pursuits. As more joined the family and they grew, too, I would try to have all my kids working with me at once. On days when we had all the time in the world, and everyone was completely well rested and nourished, and my mothering cup was completely full, it was doable and fun. But on other days when time was short or naps had been missed, it wasn't pretty and ended up with a lot of jockeying for position and me freaking out at the amount of time/space/kid-friendly tasks available and the amount of refereeing/negotiating that I needed to do. All while simultaneously trying to get a meal on the table.

To maintain the peace and get dinner on the table and feel

like I was sharing skills with my kids, something had to change. I tried giving them each their own station, which worked great for them but was somewhat of a challenge for me running back and forth between kids and tasks. I tried having them alternate in for certain tasks but that also proved to be difficult because certain tasks are just more desirable than others. I even tried letting chaos rule. But that didn't really come naturally to me.

All I knew was that I needed a plan and I wanted cooking to be productive, fun, informative, and connecting.

One evening when I was home with just one, it came to me. We were cooking together and enjoying the process and really having good conversation. It was exactly the feeling I wanted. And I realized one-on-one in the kitchen was just what we needed.

I devised a schedule wherein I'd have one child cooking with me at a time.

On their appointed night, if they wanted to help they could. If they didn't want to, that was fine, too. And even if they weren't helping it was their turn to kind of hang out in the kitchen while I cooked. All in all it made for some great time together, filled with informative conversations and surreptitious instruction— my favorite kind.

Lately it's my husband who does most of the cooking in our house. What started as a simple interest in making rice and beans has now expanded into a multinational fusion fest of tastes. Great for me, not necessarily great for young taste buds.

A Slow Family friend even shared her interpretation of one-on-one cooking with kids who are picky eaters. Carmen has three daughters. Dinnertime in her house had consistently been a bit of an issue, with her kids complaining about what was served to them and, in turn, not eating what was offered; the overall result was a very unsatisfying family time that was supposed to instead serve as a time for everyone to come together.

She created a weekly menu, planned by the group (with certain parameters of course). Each child gets a turn to help plan and cook his or her determined meal, which Carmen says has greatly reduced the amount of complaining while simultaneously increasing their whole family's pleasure around the table. They get some one-on-one cooking time. They have their weekly menu figured out ahead of time so there's no scurrying for meal ideas. The meals get eaten with fewer complaints. And dinner conversations can be about more important things than who is going to eat their potatoes. The end result is more fun, more joy, and more connection. Who doesn't want more of that?

46

How Low Can Your
Pantry Go?

It's midweek. You're tired. It's nearing dinnertime and there isn't much left in the house to make an easy supper. It's time for the big grocery store run but nobody is quite up for it. Not you, not your partner, and certainly not the kids. The last thing you want right now is another to-do on the errand list, especially a big one like food shopping.

But a family's got to eat, right?

That's all right. Take a deep breath, sit down for a few, and relax! Rather than run off to the store or run to the nearest restaurant for dinner or for takeout, you can make it into a game we call the Pantry Game. In fact, not just for tonight but for the next several nights—see just how long you can go making meals with what you've got. Not only can you put off that grocery store run you've been shrinking from for days but you can actually make it into a way of creating some slow, fun, and creative family time.

Here's the challenge.

Get everyone on board. If you've got older kids they can team up with each other or work solo, if you've got little ones, they can be a part of your team. If you've got enough to make a couple of teams, challenge each other to make different courses.

Look through your pantry, your freezer, your fridge. What's in there? Just because there isn't an easy idea, doesn't mean there isn't something good. See that homemade marmalade from your neighbor from last Christmas? Or the pork chops in the back of the freezer? What's that flat bread doing in there? And that can of beans. Get a few ingredients out and come up with your own ideas or type them in your Internet browser's search bar and see what pops up. You'll have a handful of recipes at your fingertips in no time.

Anyone can run off to the store, but it takes a family working together to come up with something good and creative and innovative. And rather than wasting time at the store, you're home all working together. No doubt laughing at some of the outcomes, too.

See how many days you can go. See if you don't feel the abundance in your life—the fact that you can go for days on end eating beautiful meals when your mind was telling you it was almost over. You'll not only get some good family time to-gether, you just might come up with the next family favorite. So hang out at home and put off that dreaded grocery store task until you can fit it in a little better. Maybe even make a date out of it!

47

Siblings for Life

Any grown-ups you know with strong sibling ties will tell you that their relationship with their siblings is one of the most influential, inspirational, and instrumental relationships they have. And at the same time, it can be one of the most loaded relationships there is.

In siblinghood we learn so much about life and about ourselves. We learn to cooperate and compromise, to fight and forgive, to share secrets and commiserate; we learn to navigate relationships and deal with our parents; and we learn how to divide something exactly evenly in the great game of I'll-split-you-pick-first.

To this day, when I am with my siblings, I feel connected from my very core. As a parent, my biggest hope for my children is that they find comfort and fun in each other and that they actually *want* to spend time together. To me, and to Kenny, too, it is one of our utmost goals.

To make sure that can happen, we offer them time alone, without us. Time for them to create their own inside jokes and share feelings. Sure, I want to jump in and know it all, but I do my best to step back and shut my mouth, even when I don't really want to.

To build this connected feeling we have sent them on airplanes together to visit relatives without us. We have signed them up for classes together and teams and sent them collectively out on errands or put them to work together at home. We try to leave them home alone where they are required to count on each other and where they can see and celebrate their differences as much as their similarities.

When we can put our children in situations in which they rely on each other, without us, the dynamics shift. They negotiate their own way, come up with their own solutions; they discuss what is needed, what is fair, what is funny, what is scary, and what is amazing, without us there to influence them. It's a nudge of connection I hope they'll feel their whole lives long.

48

Date Night

Just like family nights (only with fewer people, of course), date nights seem to get priority only if they are scheduled and written down on the calendar. If they are spoken but not written, they get usurped by the minutiae of life.

For the sake of the entire family, put it on the calendar. Then make it happen.

You don't have to go anywhere fancy or expensive, you just have to go away from the house together with the intention of spending quality time together. Undisturbed. Uninterrupted.

One night we went out on a date on a weekend night. Not our favorite time to go out because everything is crowded and overrun with people, which is not at all what we are looking for in a date night. We drove around town looking for a place to go where we could sit quietly.

Finally what we realized is that what we really wanted was to be home having a beer together on the front porch. We stopped at the store for a six-pack, drove back home, and parked down the street so nobody would hear us. We sneaked in the front gate and sat quietly in the yard, in the dark, while the sitter had the kids in the house. We had a beautiful time talking quietly and trying not to be noticed. It was a beautiful date.

And my mom would tell us all—though I haven't been so good about following this idea, but I'm trying—that all partners should go away together, too. For the fifty-plus years they were married they went away twice a year for my dad's work. They would farm us all out, and though it took a lot of prep, out we would go and off they would go for forty-eight hours or more of time alone.

Can you farm your kids out? Can you get twenty-four hours of time alone on occasion? Once a year? What's that saying about family life? All because two people fell in love . . .

And in between date nights, when you find yourselves with a few minutes alone together, try speed dating. Set a timer for ten minutes. Look each other in the eye. Touch each other in some way; hold hands, sit side by side or face-to-face. And check in.

What were your highs of the day? What were your lows? What were the surprises? Your aggravations? What do you need to move into tomorrow? Take turns sharing things you heard, things you saw. Or just spend fifteen minutes sitting with each other, breathing intentionally, if that's all you can muster.

When the timer goes off, go back to all the chores and tasks and distractions and requirements that still await.

Come on. There's always time for a quickie.

49

The Half-Full Weekend

It took us a long time to figure out how to make weekends work for us—as individuals and as a family—so that by the time Monday morning rolls around, we feel connected and refreshed, as opposed to vaguely unsatisfied and not quite rested up enough to face the new week.

What we discovered we needed was less stimulation and more incubation. Less constant weekend fun and more space to daydream, ponder, and even be a little bit bored. Less go, go, go and more chilling out at home.

For a long time, we left our weekends totally up in the air, ready to be grabbed at a moment's notice by any invitation that came our way. If we were asked, and there was a blank space on the calendar, we would respond with a ready yes—to the point that chaos ruled, and we had little say in how we spent our precious days off.

Then we realized that if one weekend day was busy with friends, errands, parties, obligations, then the next would best be left empty. No play dates, no parties, no errands to run. Just family time and yard time and house time and creativity and reading and hanging out as a family. Sometimes we'd go on a hike or a family outing outside, but more often we were home, and if we really played our cards right, car-free.

We know there might be protests each week, and sometimes we crumble to the demands of sporting events, birthday parties, and other activities. But to beat that one day at home alone together, an invitation has to be pretty darn good. Sounds like another win–win, right?

50

A Night in the Park

It is often said that it takes a village to raise a child. Without my village, I don't know where I'd be. The village works for the sake of the children so they can play and be parented by others and see that there is more than one way to live, and for the sake of the parents to have time with other parents with whom they can get ideas, share frustrations, and have some fun, too.

Nowadays many of us live away from our families and so the village must be formed. If there is any advice I can give to young families—no matter whether you are urban, suburban, rural, or somewhere in between—it is to build your tribe, find your people, create your village. And once you do, gather with them regularly for comfort, for solace, for rituals, and for fun.

Park night is all about gathering with your tribe. And it is all about comfort, solace, and joy for every single member of the family. Of course for us in a southern climate, the gathering in the park is possible year-round, but wherever you live, the key is not the location but the gathering. So call it park night or call it kitchen table night, just call it however you can.

Park night ebbs and flows sometimes happening weekly or monthly and in starts and stops. It is ritual and routine but it is not, by any stretch, mandatory.

Mostly we meet on Fridays, a perfect exclamation point to our busy week. Three or four families with a gaggle of kids of all ages. We gather in a neighborhood park, and we bring bikes, scooters, beer, food, and whatever else we need for a good time to be had by all.

We meet in the evening usually, around supper time, when most of the other families are heading home. We claim a picnic table, usually the same one week after week, and the food is spread out for one and all, each family bringing what they can and taking what they need. The beer is poured for the parents, the kids have a nibble and then run free like a pack—into the woods, along the creek, onto the swings or the not oft used lit-up tennis court.

Mostly we don't see what they do, and we like it like that. They don't ask us for input . . . usually. For the most part they are self-governing, which is one of the beauties of park night and one of the things that keeps it going.

The parents sit at the table, noshing, drinking, and talking about our week. Sometimes it is just us mamas and sometimes the dads join us, too. We get ideas, share inspirations, ask questions, and sometimes cry on each other's shoulders. We get input for parenting struggles or creative pursuits or issues we have with one thing or another. But mostly we really just have fun.

The pack of kids range in age from teen to toddler and so they need no input from us. The olders watch the youngers and the youngers watch the olders and together they skate, bike, play hide-and-seek, and sometimes even sneak in the pool on particularly hot nights. They know on these nights that the longer they remain invisible, the longer the night will continue, and so they tend to their own fights, decisions, and fallen-off bike chains.

Sometimes the teens go back and forth between the worlds: kid play and adult chat. And we welcome them in to hang on either side of the proverbial fence. It is the perfect place for them to practice being older.

So build your tribe. And gather regularly. In whatever way you can.

51

Take a Mental Picture

Life sometimes goes by faster than we can fathom. With kids in the house especially we become aware of the velocity of time. One summer they are babies, by fall they are toddlers, and seemingly overnight they become kids sitting at our tables, having conversations about homework and school applications.

It is crazy, and my mom, at age eighty-seven, tells me that sometimes life feels like a blink as she looks at where she is now and recounts working at the candy counter of the five-and-dime, going off to school, and having little babies of her own. Take it all in she says to us. Capture the moments.

As I look at my growing kids, I know what she means. Though I feel we're just starting out on this family thing, when I run into friends I haven't seen in a while the speed of time becomes evident as they say they haven't seen us since the youngest was a baby or the oldest was in kindergarten.

Children are the barometers of time's swift pace.

So how do we capture the present? How do we find the moments to pause and take it all in? How do we find ways to truly see each member of our family for who they are and where they are and where we are as a family, at each given moment?

We can take a tip from the world of technology and do something like a screen grab, freezing a moment of time. It is not an in-depth file or document, but rather a snapshot, taken with whatever camera we can put our hands on (even if it's an imaginary one).

It is not a capture of the big events such as birthdays or holidays or awards banquets and the like. But rather a mental capture of the daily minutiae. It is not a tangible thing such as a photo on a computer screen or in a book but rather a moment of extreme presence.

I pause, for just a split second, as we set the table or lie about reading books in the living room. I take a breath and stop my action as I take in kids playing in the yard or drawing a picture. It is not a memento for the future but a keepsake of the right now.

Moments that are sweet and fun and even moments that are hard, tired kids or hungry kids, fighting or overwhelmed by life, we can take a mental picture, a screen grab of our time all together under one roof.

It allows me to take it all in so that I can taste it fully while we're in it. It is like a whisper from time itself and a reminder that we are here. We are now.

And really, isn't that all we ever have?

52

Screen Free

Screens are everywhere. As a society and as a family, we use and rely on them on a daily basis. We use them from the minute we wake up, when our alarm flashes, to the minute we go to sleep, when we check weather or calendars to see what tomorrow will bring. Without a doubt, they have become a crucial part of our existence.

Personally, most days, my work is on a screen. I write on my laptop all day. I use my phone to stay in touch with clients, projects, and my family via texts, photos, and email. Whether I'm on the big screen of the computer or the small screen on my phone, it has become constant and an inevitable part of my and my family's daily existence. And, except in extreme cases, this seems to be true for most families.

For our children, too, screens play a role in their day for school, play, and rest. And while each family makes its own rules about what age is the appropriate age for a phone or whether video games come into the home or movies into the car, to escape screens completely is rare.

We know this. And we accept it, too.

As our kids have gotten older and the number of screens have increased, we felt we were heading down the slippery slope of obsessive screen time—texts chiming in, information checked, questions resolved, emails sent, recipes searched, plans made, all of it with an uncomfortable sense of modern-day urgency: Must. Do.It.Now.

So we declared, for the entire family, a screen-free time. For us it's from 5:00 to 8:00 in the evenings: screens off, phones, too; no email, games, texts, or social media. Not just for the kids, but for the entire family.

It was hard at first. And the difficulty made us realize just how much the habit had been established. If someone was trying to communicate, we needed to take action immediately. If we had a question, we wanted the answer *now*. And questions asked of us? Well, of course our expertise/insight was being called upon and so we needed to respond right away.

No matter what was going on at the time.

Another family I know, in an effort to maximize family time and minimize disconnect, has declared a screen-free zone. Whether you are adult or child, family member or guest, working or playing, if you are in the kitchen, you are off the screen. It is their family sanctuary and their homage to presence.

Before you make any rules, hours, or zones for your own family, ask yourself first how do screens impact your time together. How are they bringing you closer? And how might they be getting in the way of your time together? Ask yourself, and each other: On a scale of 1 to 10, how balanced is my screen time (1 meaning I'm on my devices so much that I'm ignoring everything going on around me, and 10 meaning I've struck the perfect balance of screen time and family time).

Ask your kids what they think. Ask your partner too and while you're at it, rate yourself. Then see how your scores compare.

Once you've figured out where you are currently with the screens and where you want to be, make a screen-free declaration that works for you—either screen-free times or zones, a combination of both, or some screen rules completely of your own creation.

53

Take Five

Sometimes you just need a break. Yes, you love your family but there are limits to how much you can take in any given day, and those limits can change from day to day. The very same act that can seem tolerable one day can drive you to the edge the next day. And sometimes you just need to walk away.

Of course in family life we don't always have that option of just heading out when we want or need to. Our family is counting on us. They need us. Our babies, our toddlers, our big kids, and our partner, too. They need to be fed, or tucked in or played with or any number of other things that may demand our attention.

So what if when their needing us and our needing a break get in the way of each other? What if we know that unless we get that imperative break we just won't be able to find the necessary joy and connection in the process?

There are some teeny things we can do that won't necessarily be a night on the town or even an hour by ourselves, but there are ways we can get the feeling of having a little time to ourselves so we don't lose our mind completely, so we can gain a little perspective, and so that we can find a little joy and connection in the many things required of us.

When my kids were little my favorite way to get a few minutes alone was with a trick I call the Garbage-Out-Fake-Out. I would grab the kitchen garbage—no matter its level of fullness. By taking the trash I was assured that nobody would follow me out. Our trash is in the alley and so it takes me a few minutes, and in this mode I would walk out as slowly as possible. I would ditch the trash then stand in the yard for a few minutes breathing in the wonderful fresh air. Face to the sun, eyes closed, deep breaths, in and out and in and out. Sometimes I would walk the perimeter of the yard and as the kids got a little older I would walk down the alley, around the half block and then back in the front gate.

If I stayed outside long enough, eventually they would come find me and then I could parent outside *way* easier than I could ever parent inside. The fresh air, the space, and the capacity to create as much noise as they wanted to made my job feel way easier—especially on those days when my tolerance was low.

Whether your children are big or small or somewhere in between, there are lots of ways you can take five or three or one minute, if that's all that you can squeeze in. And taking a little mental escape from it all can sometimes be the difference between finding some joy in the process and wallowing in the crankiness.

Here's a short list of my favorites, in order of preference. Try them out and see which ones work for you. Improvise your own and make a list to keep where you can see it—and use it—at the necessary moments.

1. Stand by your kitchen sink with feet shoulder width apart. Fill a big glass of water and drink the entire thing slowly, thoughtfully, and completely. Breathe through your nose as you do it.

2. Lie down on the floor in Child's Pose for a minute, two minutes, or more—or as long as you can before someone climbs on your back.

3. Go in the bathroom. Shut the door behind you. Stand by the window, feet wide apart, hands on top of your head. Stare outside, let your mind wander. Find a bird and follow its path. Breathe. Until someone comes knocking on the door.

4. Put a hard-backed chair in the middle of the floor. Sit in it with your back pressed against the chair, feet flat on the floor, hands to your side or on your lap. Breathe big deep breaths.

5. Remember childbirth? Use that same cleansing breath that you learned back then. In through your nose. Out through your mouth. Audibly, intentionally, deeply.

A few minutes can go a long, long way. Whether you've been home all day with the kids or you're just returning home from a long day out. We all need a little refresh every now and again.

Slow Holidays

Perhaps the hardest time of all to live your family life the way you want to live it is around the holidays. There is so much to do and so many traditions to consider and so many other people that are counting on your family doing things a certain way; the way it's *always* been done. But just because something's always been done a certain way, doesn't make it right . . .

Once upon a time there was a woman who was getting her Christmas roast in the oven. Before she put it in, she cut the end off, put it in a smaller pan and slid the two pans into the oven.

When her daughter asked her why she was doing that she told her simply, that was the way her mom did it; the way it had always been done.

The daughter then asked Grandma why the roast was always cooked in two pans. She told her simply, that was the way her mom always did it; the way it had always been done.

The little girl then went upstairs and asked her great-grandmother, and she replied, "Oh, because my oven was so small and in two pans was the only way it would fit."

As you ponder your own family holidays, think about the aspects of the holiday season that you like and the ones that drive you a little bonkers. As you ponder, realize traditions weren't always traditions. Someone had to start it sometime, and now you, as an adult and parent, also get to create your own—full of whatever traditions you want to create or emulate.

Before diving in and figuring out just what those changes might be, it's a good idea to take a look at what your childhood holidays were all about; keeping in mind that you and your partner are coming from two different experiences. Here are some questions and activities to get you started:

* What messages did you get as a child about what the holidays should look and feel like?

* What messages do you get now from society and from friends and family about what the holidays should look and feel like?

* What feelings do you want to pass on to your children about the holidays?

✳ Go back over the answers to the first three questions and sum each of these questions up in three words.

✳ Now, list five things that your own family did/does for the holidays that you *would like* to do with your family now. (Have your partner do this exercise as well.)

✳ List five things that your family did/does that you definitely *don't* want to do.

✳ How would you do each of these differently? Can you change them or eliminate them completely?

Discuss with your family how you can make new holiday traditions together. How can you unpack the old and bring in some new to make the holidays more fun, joyful, and connected for your family?

55

Out with the Old
(Before You Ring in the New)

In our household of six people, the holidays can get a bit over-whelming. Not the events so much. We've got those under control. Together we decide where we'll go, what we'll attend, which holiday events we like, and which ones can fall by the wayside.

But the influx of physical stuff—the toys, the games, the giant gifts, and other items that can quickly fill a house—is a constant challenge. And it's not just the grown-ups who begin to feel overloaded—after the holidays and birthdays pass, even the kids aren't clamoring for much more.

To keep our sanity, and our space, we have created a new holiday tradition. During the month of December, we play a little game to clear out the clutter. Each day, every member of the family is required to get rid of at least one thing. It can be something small, such as the tiny Polly Pocket shirt found under the bed, or it can be something big, such as the plastic bin full of oversize and outgrown Duplos that no one plays with anymore. It can be something you pass on to someone you know, or something you put out on the curb in the free pile. Occasionally we even have an item that is beyond redemption, and so it goes straight out the door and into the garbage.

Each of us searches through our drawers full of trinkets, under our beds, on tabletops, and in bookshelves. Every day for thirty-one days, from December 1 through December 31, we each get rid of one thing. It is a careful examination of all we have, what we need, and what we actually want in our lives. By the end of the thirty-one days, collectively we have freed up a lot of space—not just in our physical space, but in our mental capacity as well as we eliminate clutter and think about what we really need.

It feels good—fun even—as everyone makes their way through various trash and treasures, and it's enlightening to see what things hold their value for each member of the family. Try it and see.

56

Going from Fast to Slow

Families often tell me that they *want* to slow down but they don't know where they'd even begin to begin. They want to do it differently but because they've been doing it a certain way for so long, they fear it's almost impossible to change. It's too much or too hard or just too late.

Fear not. No matter how long you've been doing it one way, no matter how late you fear it might be, you can start slowing things down with just a little information, a willing heart, and a big desire.

Whether you want to slow things down for good or just for the upcoming weekend, you can. And you can start right now.

Get rid of the little voice telling you that you can't. Get rid of the excuses that keep you from beginning now. Tune out the naysayers, even if the naysayers' voices are coming from inside your own head! And get started with the following questions:

* Why do you want to slow things down?

* What are the biggest challenges in doing things the way you dream or the way you want them to be?

* What are some things you can do right away to slow down your family life? Right this minute, today, or this week?

* Is there anything you can eliminate from your schedule in the short term? A party you don't need to attend? A meeting that could be easily skipped? An extra trip to the grocery store?

* What are some things you can eliminate in the long term to slow down your family life? An extracurricular that isn't really giving you what you want? A weekly or monthly agenda item that could be easily eliminated?

* In five words or less, how do you want your family life to feel?

* How will you know when you are living your slow family life? (Hint: Go for the feeling.)

* How will you celebrate your success?

Start small if it feels overwhelming. Bite off little chunks at a time until you realize you are doing it just how you want to be doing it. If not now, when?

57

How Did We Get Here?

Sometimes in the day-to-day rush of family life, it's hard to remember where it all began. It's hard to conjure up the memories of love and miracle and wonder that were the impetus for the foundation of your family in the first place—what desires and visions led us to take a leap into the great unknown of parenthood and lifelong connection as a family.

So, in the name of getting back to that love and desire, let's forget the have-tos, and tedium, and long, sleepless hours for a moment. To refresh and renew it all so that we may continue on joyfully, ask yourself these questions:

* What are three words that describe why you decided to create a family?

* When you first realized you'd be creating a family, either at the moment your partnership began or the moment you realized you'd be adding a child, how did you feel?

* Thinking back to your early days together, think of one of your dreamiest, happiest moments as a family. Maybe it was your honeymoon, or the first days you brought your baby home, or the first time you went for a walk all together, or went on vacation, or even the first time you watched your child sleep. What were some of the feelings you had?

* What have you gained by creating a family?

* If someone were to look in on your family at that time, on your best day, what are three words he might use to describe what he saw?

* If someone were to look in on your family now, on your best day, what are three words he might use to describe what he sees?

* On those same best days, what are three words that describe how you feel?

* What are three things that make you glad to come home to your family?

* When your own child is thinking of creating a family, what is something you might tell him about the wonders of it all?

Dig deep, go back to those days of miracle and wonder, and bring a little bit of that into the here and the now.

58

Partner Up

Sometimes it's a little too easy to point out to our partners what they're doing wrong even when there are a thousand things each day that they are doing right. Sometimes it's a little too easy to focus on our own faults, too.

The questions you'll answer in this chapter are all about the strengths of your and your partner's parenting. (Ever notice that partner and parent have the same letters?) As you work through your answers you're going to figure out where you draw inspiration from your partner and where your talents lie as parents.

If you are a single parent, you can do this exercise for someone else. Perhaps you have another parent with whom you share a lot of ideas and childcare. Or maybe you have help from a grandparent or other family member. Maybe you have a trusted caregiver whom you rely on for love and support of your children and yourself as a parent.

Whomever you've got to help you along the way, now's the time to give yourselves the space to really dive deep into all the things that inspire and all the things you love, admire, and appreciate!

Ready?

* What are your strengths as a parent?

* What do you see as your partner's strengths as a parent?

* What has been the most rewarding and/or joyful thing about switching from being just partners, to being co-parents?

* What has been the hardest?

* From where do you get ideas or inspiration for your own parenting?

* What ideas and inspiration do you get from your partner about parenting?

* Where does your partner look to you for ideas or support around parenting?

* List three things you appreciate about your own parenting.

* List three things you appreciate about your partner's parenting.

* List three things you appreciate about parenting together.

59

Reflect and Project

When Carrie Contey and I began working together, we came up with a term for a writing exercise we called Projection-Reflection. It's a writing tool used to look back at the past to determine what you want for the future.

It's a great tool for gathering ideas, setting intentions, and generally figuring out what you want out of this life of ours.

In family life there is a great need to stay present, to truly be in the here and the now, and at the same time collect memories while also keeping a glimpse on the future. Depending on how old your children are now, it's sort of strange to think of our children becoming adults—yet that is precisely the goal, right? We birthed babies, but we're making future adults. And it happens really, really fast.

For this particular exercise, we're going to first look back at our own experience growing up. Then we'll flash ahead twenty years to the point when all of your existing children have reached young adulthood. Start when you're ready and have your partner answer them, too.

First, let's reflect . . .

* In your own childhood experience, what were five things you did as a family that you loved and that made you glad to be in your family? Think of mealtimes, bedtime rituals, vacations, fun, friends, and so on.

* In three words, sum up how you felt during each of those times.

* Do you do these things now with your own family? Do you want to?

Now, let's go into the future. Let your mind wander a little and get a little fantastical. It's twenty years from now. To start, write down each family member's name and age. Then answer each of the following questions in three words:

* How does your relationship with your partner feel?

* What were three things you did as a couple to foster that relationship?

* How does your relationship(s) with your child(ren) feel?

* What were three things you did as a parent to foster that (those) relationship(s)?

* How does family life with grown children feel when you all come together?

* What are your favorite things to do when you all get together as a family?

Beneath Every
Behavior Is a Need

We are often taught that to be needy is to be weak. Yet as humans we have basic needs that must be met. There are survival needs such as food, water, and shelter. There are emotional needs such as love and comfort. There are needs around safety and protection, community and learning.

And under each one of our behaviors as humans is a need. When someone in the family is upset, parents and children alike, they have a need—be it something physical or emotional. As a parent, as a human even, I'd like to say I remember this all the time, but truly, my average could be better. Much better.

Because when I do remember that under the whining or fighting or nagging or crying, there is a need, I definitely can connect easier with my children and with my partner and even with myself.

Of course everyone's needs can't always be met but we can at least acknowledge their existence, thereby meeting those needs on some level. If for example I'm impatient with my kids, my need might be food or exercise or time alone. If my kids are fighting, the need could be to be heard, to be fed, to sleep more, to have more time alone. If I can first pause, then I can figure out what the need is. From there I can find a way to meet it on some level—either right then or in the future. If the kids are resisting bed because they're in the middle of a game, they might be in need of more playtime or sibling time. It might look as if they were simply resisting, but the pause gives me the space to see the greater need. I can't necessarily grant it right then, but I can at least see it and name it, and together we can plan for it in the future. By naming the need, which even they might not realize, we can move through it.

And, just like a training muscle, the more we take time to practice, the better off we are at it. The better we are at pausing, seeing, and understanding just what our needs are.

So here's a little game you can play to practice seeing the need beneath the behavior.

At home with your family, take some time to just observe. At the dinner table, after school, before bed, or hanging in the yard, just observe.

As you observe, ask yourself first, what is the behavior? Second, what is the need under the behavior? Try it on your partner and your kids. What do they need they're not getting? What need are they expressing with whatever they are doing? It could be joyful behavior or sad or mad or crazy. And underneath it all there is some express need. Play it with your partner even making it into a little friendly speculative competition.

Use this approach with your own behavior, too. Next time you are crying, laughing, yelling, or freaking out, pause and ask yourself first, What is the behavior? And second, What is the need beneath the behavior? Then figure out a way to satisfy it.

61

The Family Billboard

In the virtual world I receive little inspirations throughout the day—through newsletters that I subscribe to, social feeds, or items friends send me. They are sometimes sentimental, sweet, funny, and always inspiring. I of course forward the ones I like to spread the inspiration far and wide.

At home I wanted to share ideas, too, without the need to always be talk, talk, talking and without the need for everyone to have a screen in front of them. I have finally found the place to put it where I am sure to have a captive audience.

In the bathroom I have affixed a plastic file sleeve to the wall across from the toilet. It is not the fanciest thing I have ever created but it is utilitarian in design and completely effective in its usage.

It is not a place for appointment reminders or other calendar events, rather it is a place where I can forward onto my family all the inspirations I receive throughout the day—and even make up some of my own.

I leave notes to the family about revelations I've had. I leave prose pertinent to something we might be experiencing as a family or comics that are relevant to our current situation. I leave diagrams detailing tasks that need doing or lessons learned or short pieces about struggles we might be having or dynamics we have fallen into. I post poetry and short essays and drawings and flow charts and all kinds of things to inspire us as a family as we make our way through our days both together as a family and in the world at large.

After something has hung for a while or when I come across something new or when we shift into a new dynamic, I simply slide it out and insert the next.

It's become a great tool for sharing my messages with my family without having to gather everyone together or ask for quiet or make sure they're mentally ready to receive. It's a way for them to know what's on my mind without having to comment or critique. And it's a way too for me to quietly share a thought, idea, or inspiration without having to interrupt the normal flow of family life.

The location means that when each person is reading, they are alone, with no disturbances or disruptions to the chain of thought.

After something has hung for a while I might ask about it or discuss it, after they have had time to digest and ponder whatever is posted there.

It's like my own little billboard on which I can advertise all the things that I feel are important to us as a family.

And as the kids got older they started leaving things there, too, messages for us all or drawings. That's how I know it's working.

62

Real Cooperation

Often parents think of cooperation as another way of saying their child is obedient, doing what the parent wants. If kids are cooperating, it means they are doing what we ask them to do. Think about the word itself, though. It means not "to be subservient" but "to *work together.*"

What if we approached more of family life cooperatively? What if, instead of a kid having to clean her own room or a parent having to clean the kitchen after supper, the family worked together? The work would not only get done faster but the family would find more connection in the process, too.

What if, instead of a kid taking guitar lessons, the lessons were cooperative so that the parent who was chauffeuring the kid to lessons was also learning how to play, or the sibling who was dragged along was getting a lesson, too?

And if one child did get a lesson on his own, what if part of his practice meant that he taught a sibling or a parent the thing he was practicing? Wouldn't he learn it better if he had to not only do it but teach it?

How about if you were confused about what to do as a parent, and you turned to your kids and asked them what they thought about it? What if you told them that you really didn't know what to do when people fought or when clothes were left all over the floor or if people didn't do the jobs that were assigned to them? What if, instead of thinking that as a parent you had to know all the answers, which seemed to be always changing anyway, you asked for input from your kids and friends?

Sometimes as parents we think we're supposed to know it all, but what if we approached our challenges cooperatively instead, asking those around us to give us a hand?

63

Dance Party Rock Band

When you want to shake off the day, spark a little creative fun time, get everybody moving, and let off a little familial steam all at the same time, there is nothing like a little good, loud music and a big, clear dance floor.

Leave the dinner dishes where they are and head to the biggest room in the house. Push all the furniture to the side. Get the chairs and tables and tchotchkes out of the way. And crank up the music as loud as you can.

After you've all had a little time to get loose and really feel the groove, circle up and start calling out some themes, roller rink style. Call out some wild moves like "shaky arms" or "crazy legs" or some other random suggestions that leave plenty of room for interpretation like "apple pie" or "ice cream sandwich."

Call out different animals or plants and let everyone take turns giving their best dance interpretation of the given theme.

There's no judging. No best in show. Just moving it, feeling it, and taking a little time for some family dance interpretations.

If you've got instruments in the house, break those out, too. Play along, either for real or for pretend. Claim an instrument and a role in the band or let your kids orchestrate who gets what. Maybe you're tambourine or maybe you're lead guitar; either way you get to be in the family band. Play for a while then switch it up, just keep the momentum going.

Give everyone a turn to go solo on the dance floor. Let them show off some of their best moves; let everyone have a turn to shine while everyone else provides the cheers.

Let yourself go. Let loose. Set your mind free, and let your body really and truly feel the beat of the music. No holds barred. No fear of judgment. No worries that you're doing it wrong because in a family dance party there is no wrong!

Have a few playlists ready to go so that when the mood strikes you, you can find the mix that best suits the family's mood. If you have older kids, let them make a mix.

Call out a family dance party whenever the mood seems right. Use this method in the winter when cabin fever is at its height. Or in the summer when the doldrums and heat combine to cause a bit of familial malaise. Call it when you're solo parenting or when you need a reason to celebrate. Use it to adjust attitudes or when you just feel the need to shake things up a little.

When you get the music pumping and you're surrounded by

the people you love the most in this world, celebrate as a group. On the dance floor, you can feel the joy of being part of the best music group in the world—in your body, in your mind, and in your spirit, too. And once you've got it going, it can carry you for a long, long time!

64

Spontaneous Game Night

It's almost bedtime. It's time to tuck the kids in and get ready for another day of school, work, or whatever you've got on your plate the next morning. The kids are all jammied and brushed, and you're *this close* to a little rest and relaxation. So close you can practically taste it!

Just as the kids are heading to bed, turn them around and march them right to the kitchen table. Set the timer for twenty minutes and break out the Bananagrams or Pictionary or any other game that can be played in short bursts (no Candy Land or Monopoly, please!). It's time for a Slow Family quickie. (No, not that kind.)

Before you begin, explain the rules. When the timer goes off, the game is over. No matter what point you're at. At that moment, it's time for bed, and any needs that need meeting should be met now, before the game starts. When it's time for bed, it's time for bed. No ifs, ands, or buts. And those who want to play have to promise they will try their hardest to wake up cheerfully in the morning. Tell them too that if this little bonus time works out for everyone, you'll call for it on a regular and random basis. And as you *shoosh* them off to bed at the end of the game, make it silly and fun and give it a "go, go, GO!!" energy.

Watch their eyes pop when you tell them not to go to bed.

Watch yourself relax when you realize you're giving them this bonus time only to have fun together as a family.

And watch this little fifteen- or twenty-minute game bring you all together, for one last little dose of family time before you head off to bed.

It's as simple as that.

Rather than go to bed with everyone focused on his or her own process and own self, enjoy the connection of everyone sitting at the table together.

Rather than feel a little frenzied and frazzled, enjoy a little fun all together.

Don't worry about the twenty minutes or so later bedtime.

Don't worry that you're breaking the normal schedule.

Just look at your beautiful family.

And realize that you can do this only now. And that in the grand scheme of life, twenty minutes less sleep isn't going to hurt anyone, but twenty minutes extra for family time, stolen from the regular routine, sitting at a table and playing a game all together, could bring you a connection that your children will remember their whole lives long.

And truly, when they're grown, and reflecting on their childhood with their own children, they will remember those moments when their parents let them stay up late on a school night to play a game. They won't remember that it was only twenty minutes. They won't even remember that you may have done it only a few times a year. They'll remember that you sat at the table all together and played a game when a game wasn't even on the agenda!

Fun, right?

65

The Family Lemonade Stand

Sometimes it's hard to just be. It's hard to schedule nothingness when the rest of the family wants somethingness. Maybe you want to hang out at home, doing nothing together as a family while your kids want to see someone or go somewhere or do, do, do! Though your intentions are good and your desire is strong to slow down and enjoy some family time, you might need to reframe it to meet their demands.

Enter the family lemonade stand.

Plan it out or make it spur of the moment, depending on your family's needs. Make fresh squeezed or doctor up a can or jar of store bought. Make an elaborate booth or simply set a table out on the sidewalk. Spend days making crazy, creative posters to put out on the street or make a simple marker sign minutes before you sell your first cup. The point of it all is to enjoy a little downtime at home, while giving the resident extroverts a piece of the social action.

In our neighborhood, when we hang out on the front sidewalk, we are amazed at how many neighbors we see that we never encounter otherwise. We get news of all the goings-on, and we occasionally even meet someone nearby whom we never met before. We find out about new babies and birds' nests and about property taxes and parking restrictions.

We let the kids run the show, pouring drinks, taking money, and making deals while we simply sit back and enjoy. Sometimes we dabble in yard work or a minor repair and still other times we simply sit and observe and enjoy our time hanging with the kids and chitchatting with passersby.

Of course it's a great way to teach your kids about money and entrepreneurship as you discuss costs and profits and the basics of supply and demand. The kids can feel what it's like to be a boss and determine just what wage needs to be paid to the resident five-year-old or whether she should be paid in product instead. You can make it a fund-raiser and decide all together which cause matches your family's interests and values. You can dream up ways to spend the earnings or ponder things to save for or determine just how you'll share what you make.

If you think lemonade is too cliché, sell handmade bookmarks or clay sculptures or drawings or even advice or good ideas.

Let the lessons teach themselves. Let the kids interact with the world while you enjoy a Saturday afternoon at home and the chance to hang out lazily with your kids; everyone getting what they need.

It's more than just lemonade. It's family time with a twist.

66

The Love Pop-In

I had to pop in to my kids' school one morning to drop off some papers at the office. I planned on just running in and then running back out to get back to work as quickly as possible. It wouldn't take but a minute or two.

As I headed out the front door of the building, however, I thought about my children, who were on that campus, in their respective classrooms, and who had no idea I was even there. Though I had a pretty tight schedule that day, I ran back in and beelined for my son's classroom.

I knocked and waited. Another student answered and in my most serious, earnest tone so as to imply some urgent matter, I asked to have a word with my son.

I stood back from the door, out of sight of the rest of the

class, and as he came out the door and around the corner, I attacked him with full-on hugs and kisses—making sure beforehand of course that nobody was watching so as not to embarrass him. I held his face, looked him in the eye, and said, "Hello! I just wanted to see you!" He laughed, then looked around warily, also making sure nobody was watching. He asked what I needed and I hugged him again telling him that was all. Just a hug and a hello. We then said good-bye, and away he went, back into his world and I into mine.

From there I ran to my daughter's classroom and did the same, a hug and a hello with few words. No questions, no requests, no needs for either of us other than to feel the love.

Then off I went, with a total time estimate of about six extra minutes out of my day and my heart pumping full of endorphins and connection. The speed of it all made me feel a little giddy, and I wondered how many other times and ways we could grab that little bit of connection that takes only minutes out of our day.

Could we steal five minutes from our day to create this feeling? Not that I want to interrupt my day or my kids' day on a regular basis but every now and again? In the name of love? Where could we make it happen?

We could walk our partner to the car in the morning instead of saying good-bye from the rushed state of the kitchen. We could jot off a text to our loved ones midday, sending a little love their way and letting them know simply that they are on our mind. We could dial them up for a three-minute face-to-face video chat—not to ask them to pick something up or to remember some event, but simply to say, Hey there, I love you. We

could write a small note for our children or doodle a little drawing and put it inside their lunch telling them something we appreciate about them or recounting a funny moment we shared or
identifying something they do that blows our minds.

Because really, in the big picture of family, love, joy, and connection, isn't that the real urgent matter? I think that's what
anyone who's lived awhile would tell us.

67

Freaky Friday

Ever wish you could *not* be in charge of all the decision making for your family? Do your kids ever wish they *could* be in charge? It's wearisome on both sides of the coin. And there is definitely an element of the grass being greener on the other side.

Want to turn things around a little? Even out the family playing field a little bit? And give the kids a chance to be in charge every once in a while?

Try this little game called Freaky Friday Slow Family Style.

For a couple of hours, or for an entire day, switch roles.

How you play the game depends on the age of your children, your comfort level, the amount of time you have on your hands, and, perhaps the biggest of all, your ability to let go.

But I guarantee in the end, you'll have a little fun, a greater connection to each other, and a greater understanding too of what it's like to be in each other's shoes. As a parent you might learn too that many of the things we think are so crucial really can be let go of. At least every now and again.

If you're playing with little kids, keep it simple. You might start on a walk and let them decide what direction you'd like to go. Before you hit the streets draw an arrow on a piece of cardboard that they can point in whatever direction they want to go. They'll get a kick out of being in charge of you and making a decision that affects the whole family.

If your kids are a little bit older, make the stakes a little higher. Put the whole day before them from the morning breakfast to the nighttime tuck in and everything in between. What will you eat, where will you go, what chores will you do, and if you're brave enough, even what you'll wear that day!

Let go of expectations about outcome and truly revel in the fact that the decisions are out of your hands.

It might be kind of hard at first, to let the kids take charge but the more you do it, the easier it'll be. And the more you and your children can trust the process.

It's a confidence builder on both ends. And a real lesson in figuring out just what's important and what's not. And it'll put you both in a position of walking in each other's shoes—you the decision maker, they the decided.

The following day, have a little family recap and discuss the highs and lows of it all. What did you all like? What didn't you? What things could you possibly trade on a more regular basis? And what did you all learn about each other that maybe you didn't know before?

DEAR (Drop Everything and Read) Time

I was introduced to DEAR time by my children's teachers. I didn't know it was a known acronym—I thought she made it up. It stands for "drop everything and read." And it dawned on me recently that just as it's an effective method for getting kids into reading, it's also a perfect tool for slowing things down at home. And a great way for us all to give ourselves permission to step back into a little bit of stillness.

It's about as simple as it sounds. When you are all home together, on a weekend or holiday. When the house is buzzing, people are moving, talking, and getting a little bit antsy. When your mind is on overload from the endless tasks that need tending or you see the kids are heading toward wild restlessness that can lead only to some "accidental" kick in the head, call for a DEAR time. It's like time-out. Only with a book.

You can do it as a group and read aloud from a picture book or chapter book. You can all retreat into your own little spaces, each heading off to your bed or room or a private space somewhere in the house. You can head outside onto blankets laid out on the grass. Or you can all retreat to one big room in the house and layer up on couches and floors and chairs so you can spend some time being together but all being into your very own story.

Try it after dinner too in that time before bed that can sometimes get a little wacky. Or you can call it just because you need a little break from the melee that is the norm in many households.

Let your kids pick the book. Do it regularly, and you're not only creating a culture of reading but you're giving yourself permission to just step away from all the tasks and take a little time for reading that doesn't involve falling asleep on the pillow.

Go ahead. Call for a little DEAR time in your house. Everyone will be glad you did.

Happy Birthday to You!

For a child, there is nothing quite so magical as a birthday. It is her day to celebrate life itself. To celebrate being born and be celebrated by everyone in her life. It is a day all about her.

While a big part of the birthday is of course the presents and the packages and the parties, the true celebration of the birth of a human, and the start of a family, is nothing short of magical.

The week before a birthday, we do a seven-day countdown—each day recalling something the birthday boy or girl learned in the past year and something he or she wants to do/have/try in the year ahead. It's a great process for reflecting on just how much this past year has held and also a great way to keep away the angst of waiting, waiting, waiting for the big day to arrive.

Then, to start the day off with a celebratory bang and an

honoring of the passing of time and the growth of the individual, my husband and I make a family birthday table. The night before the birthday, after the kids are sound asleep, the making of the birthday table begins.

We start by crafting a paper crown made from brown bags turned inside out and decorated with collage, crayons, buttons, photos, and paint. We clear the kitchen table of the detritus of family life and lay out a beautiful dresser scarf that came from my grandmother. We place the crown front and center, and around it put photos of the birthday celebrant taken over the years—baby pictures, of course, and a sampling from each of the years since. We mix in photos of the child with each parent and with his or her siblings. We put a big candle in the middle, a vase of flowers if we have them, small sculptures made by the celebrant and other random but special items that make the table look like a small altar. And when it is decorated to our liking, we place one small wrapped gift in the front.

While the table itself is created for the birthday boy or girl, the decorating of the table, in the quiet of a sleeping house, has become a time for Kenny and me, as parents, to really ponder the wonder and incredibleness of this human being we created together. As we work together, we remember the day our child joined our family and think about just how crazy and amazing it is that this person, who is growing before our very eyes, came to us in newborn form. And every day since has made our family, our family. Without that child's humor and words and ideas and essence, we would be a different family.

It's mind blowing. And as we speak and laugh and cry and

remember all the years thus far and ponder all the years to come, we feel our hearts opening and our connection as a family growing beyond belief.

Sure, it looks like a simple birthday table. But it is so much more! What are your family's birthday traditions? Do you carve out enough time in preparation to get beyond the practical planning so you can truly celebrate?

Lazing About

Don't Beat 'Em, Join 'Em!

It can sometimes drive parents a little nutty when kids are lazing about, flopping all over the house going from couch to bed to floor and back to couch. All the while moaning about how bored they are or how they need a friend or a movie or a something.

Society's message has long been that idle hands are, well, the start of bad things. And while this has long been the standing message, in modern times, it is actually harder than ever to flop about idly because there is always an electronic device within reach, be it phone, tablet, TV, video game, or computer.

So what if instead of talking them out of it, we actually encouraged it?

What if when our kids flopped, lazed, and whiled away the hours, instead of telling them to engage in something, we actually encouraged them to just laze about some more? Without electronics, that is.

And what if instead of discouraging such slothful behavior, we actually sidled up to them on occasion and joined them in their pursuit of random laziness.

It's not as easy as it sounds!

Say it's your family's electronics-free time. You're making supper or paying bills or sweeping or whatever it is you do during that time. Your child is floating from soft piece of furniture to soft piece of furniture, perhaps grunting, sighing, and generally being bored practically to tears, or at least to the point of harassing you that he's, ugh, bored.

Drop your broom. Turn off the stove. Put the paperwork away. And lie down next to him. Sigh exaggeratedly. Moan a big, long, deep, guttural moan from the very depths of your belly. Let it out. With great bored theatrics.

Just see what kind of reaction you get. Lie there awhile. Close your eyes. And just feel whatever it is you're feeling. Ask your children what they're feeling. Ask them where the feeling is in their body. Ask them again, how they're feeling right now. And right now. And right now.

Then pose some crazy questions. Ask them to invent a machine that grants every wish. What would it look like? What would they wish? Ask them if they could change how they felt, how would they want to feel? What would make them feel like that? Ask them their big ideas about life, liberty, and the pursuit of happiness. Ask them what they want in a friend, in life, in a parent. Ask them what would make their dreams come true. Ask them about their best friend. What makes that friend fill that role so well? Ask what makes a good friend. Ask them if they feel like they're a good friend. Seize the moment of malaise to tap into their amazing psyches.

The rest will wait. And you can create some pretty big, deep connections in just fifteen minutes or so of lazing, flopping, and dreaming together. Who knows what amazing ideas you'll come up with?

71

Don't Sweep Until the Rice Dries

When my oldest child was born, my sister Alma and my brother Damien told me, "Don't sweep until the rice dries." As the mother of a nursing infant, I didn't really get it. As my daughter got bigger and moved to the high chair, and I went to clean under her chair after a meal of rice and peas, it hit me like a thud. I got it as I struggled with the broom and the wet rice on the floor.

They meant it literally, in part. Don't try to sweep up the moist rice on the kitchen floor or it will just roll along and stick to your broom and smear rice marks on the wood and you'll end up on your hands and knees picking up each little piece of rice one at a time. Don't do it now. Just wait. Walk away. Go play on the living room floor, go for a walk outside, be with your family, play, relax, breathe. Because if you do this task now, it will take three times longer than if you just wait, and do it when it's all dried up.

It has become the perfect metaphor for slow family living. Don't choose the struggle. Don't make work for yourself. Don't make it harder than it needs to be, because when we give the struggles some space, they are much more likely to work themselves out or at least be more workable when we return.

When we take the necessary pause, the answers present themselves. When we are willing to walk away rather than let the frustration get the best of us, we can find solutions in the space we allow. And when we are willing to let others walk away, too, rather than engage the argument, then the calm, cool, connection can present its beautiful little self.

So in the literal sense, don't sweep until the rice dries. It's messy and gunky and really, really frustrating.

And in the figurative sense, don't think everything needs to be resolved right away. Give it time. Give it pause. Give tempers room to cool and moods time to swing. Then go back, when things have settled a bit and the resolutions are within easy grasp.

Give it all some space: the struggles, the work, the people, the frustrations, the overwhelm, yourself. When you do, you just might find that everything is quite manageable after all, and you'll be in a much better state of mind to deal.

72

Capturing the Ideal

Here's a simple and rather satisfying exercise to help you figure out what really works for you and your family and how you can create more of it. Capture the Ideal solo and then have your partner do it solo as well. Bring your answers together and see how they match up. If you've got older kids, it's also quite fun to have them work through the process.

* When does family life feel the most satisfying? List as many as you can.

* Think of a day, hour, or moment when you felt, "Ah!!! This is what family life is all about! This is the ideal! This is the way I dreamed it could be!"

* Describe it in detail.

* What was the feeling you had?

* What were the elements or the pieces involved?

* Can you create more of that in daily life (not necessarily the exact scenario, but the pieces that can then create the feeling)?

Here's an example to get you going . . .

In our family, we figured out some of our most ideal moments were during family road trips. No matter how long or short, we all love a family road trip. Sure, there is always a bit of jockeying for seats and figuring out which music to listen to, but overall, we all agreed, pure magic.

The feelings we have during a road trip, collectively and individually, are relaxation, fun, exciting, easy, satisfying, and content.

When we broke it down into elements, what we got was that we were all together without distraction of chores or errands or outside influence. We had a cooler full of good food. We each had our favorite books and music. We played games together and also had solo time for chilling or reading and just daydreaming and gazing out the window.

So how could we create that at home? We could set aside chunks of time for family games, we could hang out in the yard with lunch, books, and lounge chairs. And we made sure that when we were doing this at home that we took time away from all the tasks and to-dos to concentrate simply on the daydreaming and the gazing at the sky.

Try it with your family. What's your ideal? How do you get the feeling you all need and want? And what are the elements necessary to re-create the feeling in whatever way you possibly can?

73

Road Trip!

Of course, it's not always possible to be slow and connected and to really take time to see all the members of your family. There are lots of things going on and schedules to tend to, and as kids get older and take on their own activities and jobs and other commitments, family time can get harder and harder to maintain.

If you feel like it's been awhile since you've all been in the same room together or since you've laid eyes on more than one family member at a time, it's time for some familial incubation.

Enter: the Slow Family Road Trip.

Whether you have one day or a few, the family road trip can serve as an incubator for your family, giving you ample time together to talk, create, dream, and explore new ideas. And at the same time give you a little glimpse of the world around you.

And while the road trip itself is the key to it all, the prep time also holds some rather golden moments of building family connection.

Before you hit the road, call a family meeting to discuss destinations. Where will you go? How long will you drive? What's to see on the other end? Whom might you visit along the way? And perhaps most important, what snacks do people want for the ride?

At the meeting, break out some maps for everyone to peruse. Though I'm a fan of the GPS for directions, in this case a paper map can give you a good glimpse at the big picture. For the ultimate connection and relaxation, bypass the highways and instead try to find your way on the historic highways or small town roads. Without semis and eighty-mile-per-hour speeds, the smaller roads definitely allow for more slow travel and less distraction for the driver.

Allow enough space in the travel plans for stopping at random locations for swimming, exploring, and pausing wherever and whenever the desire strikes.

As you drive, play word games like twenty questions, make lists of the license plates you see, and take turns as DJ to give everyone a glimpse into each other's musical tastes. Learn songs you can all sing together—break out the old campfire favorites or have your kids teach you something modern. Print out lyric sheets so everyone can sing along in old-fashioned-karaoke style. Listen to an audio book the whole family will enjoy—a classic perhaps or a new favorite selected by one of the kids.

Pack up a cooler of good food with a good dose of healthy

snacks and intermittent sweet treats thrown in the mix. Use some otherwise forbidden foods to keep spirits up, as in, "When we hit the two-hundred-fifty-mile mark we'll bust out the Swedish Fish."

Use seat rotations to give everyone a chance at seeing the world from a different perspective. And have the kids serve as navigator at different intervals to teach them the fine art of map reading.

Sit in the back with your kids while your partner drives. Let the big kids ride in the front for a change. Turn your phone off. Stare out the window and just listen while your kids chat away. Enjoy the fact that you are all there together with no chance of escape and no need for anything other than what's going on in the car.

Whether you go across the country or around the block, intentional time in the car, with the ride being the goal, can give you just the calm, present, connected, fun time together your family needs.

74

May the Circle Be Open

When our children are small, some part of us thinks that this is how life will always be—all of us forever in each other's daily lives; tending, chauffeuring, feeding, overseeing, and generally in charge of the where, what, why, and how of our children's lives.

And then, seemingly suddenly, they are grown. And gone off to live lives of their very own.

I'm not there yet with my own children, but of course I am there in relation to my parents and siblings, all of us living in different houses, towns, states, and even countries.

As adults we are lucky to gather annually with our partners and children and some of us with our children's children. Keeping the family circle open and unbroken has been a continuous quest of ours.

We come together to refill our proverbial cups, to check in with each other, and to get support where we need it on matters of the heart, mind, and body. We feel lucky to have each other, and we look forward to our meetings each year with excitement and anticipation.

To me, it is the quintessential goal of creating a family in the first place—the desire to be together and joy in the process of gathering. And, though we were born into it, we all agree there are elements that can be created by other families, too.

Think about your own extended family of grown-up parents and siblings. When did you gather last? Where could you gather again? If you do gather, are there things you could do to make it easier and more fun? Are there issues you could let go of? What are the sticky points and how could they be unstuck? Are there perhaps apologies that could be made for grievances past? Or methods of communication that could be engaged to make it peaceful? Could judgment be suspended at least for the time you are together? Would there be benefits in getting together that would far outweigh whatever hardships might come up?

If you don't think it's possible currently, start pondering what you'd like gatherings to look like when your children are grown. Think now about what makes it hard for you to gather with your own extended family and determine how you might alleviate that issue for your own children and their partners and children. Start circling up now with your children on random occasions so that coming together in a circle is just a part of who you are as a family.

When you do gather—be it next month with your siblings or

twenty years from now with your children, here are a few ways to make it more connected and more fun:

1. Circle up. Sit together in a circle so that everyone can see everyone. Go around the circle sharing high points, news, or projects pending. Sing together. Reminisce.

2. Judge not. We all like different things. Honor this and accept the differences in the group.

3. Say what you need. If everyone says what they need, there is no room for speculation. And usually we find that others can be kind of helpful in getting our needs met.

4. Don't worry about the minutiae. Focus instead on the people, with connection being the goal.

5. Hug lots. When you are laughing, crying, fighting, or feeling just plain apathetic, hug.

6. Let go. Let go of blame, being right, being first, and being in control.

7. Listen. Talk. Inspire and be inspired.

8. Celebrate the fact that you are a loving, joyful, connected family.

75

Making Big Change

You've asked yourself the question, Is this working? And you realize it's time for something to give, or shift, to be added or to go away. You're committed. You're ready. So how do you institute the necessary change(s) so that you can really make it stick?

Years ago, Carrie Contey and I held a class on setting new intentions in your life. In it we talked about the need for stating purposes and meanings for your days. We discussed the difference between intentions and to-dos, and we went over the ways that setting new intentions and stating how you want to feel and approach things can really change your overall outlook.

As you revisit the entries in this book, you may spot ideas that strike you, approaches and activities that you might want to try, or that simply inspire you to do something differently. While the decision to change things may come easy, sometimes the implementation can be a bit more difficult.

I suggest you move slowly (no surprise!) as you change things up. Discuss them with your partner and your kids (if they are old enough). And give yourself time to try ideas on for size and see how they fit your family. Use the following ten steps that Carrie and I created to help you make the changes you want to make—slowly, thoughtfully, and without major shock to your family's system. The more room you give each change, the more likely it will be to stick.

1. Ask yourself, Why are we doing this? Are you doing it for your family or because other people say or think you should?

2. Before you begin to create any real change, it's necessary to acknowledge and examine your own ambivalence. Only you can decide which part of you is ready and which part of you isn't quite there yet.

3. Even if you are holding on to ambivalence, the commitment to change must be made before you embark.

4. Decide on the outcome you want: really imagine it happening; take time to visualize. If you can't see it and feel it, it's probably not time.

5. Talk to your child/partner/family about the change. Don't just start without informing those who will be affected.

6. Look at life and what is coming up, and make sure you are in a place/position to settle into making the necessary change in a slow and mindful manner.

7. Give it time to become a new habit. Determine how long you are willing or able to give it. Recognize that change can't necessarily come overnight.

8. Continuously assess and ask, Is this working for us?

9. If it's not time to make a change, you can still be planting the seeds by creating and stating affirmations of where you want to go. It's important to recognize that where you are right now is where you need to be right now and right now only. There will be time for change down the road.

10. No matter what you decide to do or which phase you are at in the process, appreciate where you are and what you've got going on. Feel a grateful presence for what is, which is sort of the point of this whole thing anyway.

Final Note

I hope that you have found inspiration in these pages. I hope that you have discovered at least one idea, one step, one task, one person, one change, one idea, one practice that will help you and your family slow down, connect, and truly enjoy this family life of yours, for now and for your whole lifetime together.

Acknowledgments

First and foremost, I would like to thank my mom and dad, Liz Rienzo Noll and Dean Noll, who gave me life and who gave me my eight amazing siblings. Without your love and intention, none of this would exist. Thank you for having us! And thank you for giving us your home as an incubator each summer.

To my beautiful, bird-loving, creative, and capable husband, Kenny, who entered into this family life with me, sort of blindly but mostly trusting of the process. Thank you for your willingness to dive into big family life with me—both with my siblings and extended family and with our own four children. It's not always been a smooth path, but it's certainly been adventurous!

To my four amazing children who suffer my experiments, singing, and random rituals, and who are completely honest with me in regards to what works and what doesn't. Thank you for joining me in this lifetime. You make it all worthwhile.

To my sisters and brothers—Gabriella, Alma, Ave, Thaddeus, Justin, Damien, Gregory, and Loretta. Our summer gatherings to discuss life, liberty, and the constant pursuit of happiness are the lifeblood of my year. I am renewed by our time together and am delighted that there is a piece of all of you in the whole of me.

To Alma, my godmother and big sister, I miss you and feel your presence with me always.

To the partners of said brothers and sisters, the out-laws. Especially you Melani, my constant guidance counselor.

To all of my nieces and nephews who are the first people I ever saw go from baby to adult. I am so grateful you exist and I am so happy to know you.

To Goodness, as individual women and as an entity, from and with whom I have gained so much insight over the last seven years. You provide ideas, inspiration, and serve as such loving witnesses. Thank you.

And to Carrie Contey, PhD, my cofounder of Slow Family Living, my friend, sister, guide, sometimes therapist, and willing accomplice in diving into the muck and the beauty and getting to the heart of it all. You are a dream come true.

To my agent, Laurie Abkemeier, for helping me bring this idea to the table. And to my editor, Marian Lizzi, who is making sure my ideas are presented as clearly and inspirationally as they can possibly be.

Thanks to the Twin Oaks Branch of the Austin Public Library, which provided me with a quiet and beautiful place to sit, and to Once Over Coffee Bar, which served up the most beautiful and delicious coffee a girl could ever dream of.

Finally, thanks to all the kids, parents, and families who have provided me with ideas and suggestions for this book: Kathie, Lynn, Liz, Andrea, Lara, Amy Walker, Noelle Victor Brandaw, Katy Dailey, Gabriella, Carmen Ramirez McFarlin, Elena, and all of you whose names are not here but whose support is. Thank you.

About the Author

Bernadette Noll is the mother of four, one of nine children, New Jersey native, writer, teacher, crafter, extrovert, collaborator, and coauthor of the book *Make Stuff Together*, which was published by Wiley Publishing in March 2011. She is the cofounder of Slow Family Living, which was started in an effort to help families find ways to slow down, connect, and enjoy family life. She lives in Austin, Texas, with her husband, Kenny Anderson, and their four children, Lucy, Otto, Esme, and Dean.